The Ungovernable City

MIT Studies in American Politics and Public Policy
Jeffrey Pressman and Martha Weinberg, general editors

The Ungovernable City:
The Politics of Urban Problems and Policy Making

Douglas Yates

The MIT Press
Cambridge, Massachusetts, and London, England

Eighth printing, 1991

First MIT Press paperback printing, 1984

This book was set in V-I-P Optima by The MIT Press Media Department Computer Composition Group and printed and bound in the United States of America

Library of Congress Cataloging in Publication Data

Yates, Douglas, 1944–
     The ungovernable city.

     (MIT studies in American politics and public policy ; 3)
     Includes bibliographical references and index.
     1. Municipal government—United States. 2. Policy sciences. I. Title.
II. Series.
JS341.Y38   352'.008'0973   77–11201
ISBN 0–262–74013–3 (paper)

To James W. Fesler,
teacher, colleague, friend

Contents

Editors' Foreword

Social scientists have increasingly directed their attention toward defining and understanding the field of public policy. Until recently public policy was considered to be a product of the actions of public institutions and as such was treated as the end point in analysis of the governmental process. But in recent years it has become clear that the public policy-making process is infinitely more complex than much of the literature of social science would imply. Government institutions do not act in isolation from each other, nor is their behavior independent of the substance of the policies with which they deal. Furthermore, arenas of public policy do not remain static; they respond to changes in their political, organizational, and technical environments. As a result, the process of making public policy can best be understood as one that involves a complicated interaction between government institutions, actors, and the particular characteristics of substantive policy areas.

The MIT Press series, *American Politics and Public Policy*, is made up of books that combine concerns for the substance of public policies with insights into the working of American political institutions. The series aims at broadening and enriching the literature on specific institutions and policy areas. But rather than focusing on either institutions or policies in isolation, the series features those studies that help describe and explain the environment in which policies are set. It includes books that examine policies at all stages of their development—formulation, execution, and implementation. In addition, the series features studies of public actors—executives, legislatures, courts, bureaucracies, professionals, and the media—that emphasize the political and organizational constraints under which they operate. Finally, the series includes books that treat public policy-making as a process and help explain how policy unfolds over time.

Douglas Yates's book *The Ungovernable City* looks closely at the relationship between the structure and functions of big city governments and the policies those governments produce. During the 1960s and early 1970s, scholars and citizens alike assumed that cities could be saved by enlightened political leaders who understood the urban areas they governed. Yates examines the bases and consequences of this assumption and looks at the dilemmas it has posed. He explains how the kinds of goods and services that city governments must deliver influence the expectations of both citizens and government officials and at the same time shape the environment in which political leaders operate. In addition to analyzing the question of what combination of factors makes American cities ungovernable, Yates ties his work to the existing scholarly literature and presents a new framework for studying urban politics and public policy.

Professor Yates is at the School of Organization and Management, Yale University.

Jeffrey Pressman
Martha Weinberg

Preface

In choosing the title, *The Ungovernable City*, I have consciously joined a debate that has been underway for some time and that has been highlighted by the publication of two books with similar titles, Edward Banfield's *The Unheavenly City* and Norton Long's *The Unwalled City*.[1] Each book develops an argument about what is wrong with the city and about what might be done to alleviate urban policy problems. This book also develops such arguments. But my arguments are different, for I wish to identify a different source of urban problems and a different strategy for dealing with them.

The message of the book is evident in the title. I believe that the city problem is a problem of government, that the large American city is increasingly ungovernable, and that the only solution to the problem lies in a redefinition and restructuring of urban government.

In what follows I develop an analysis of the ungovernable city in a way that is quite different from the approaches taken by Professors Long and Banfield. I will combine an analysis of urban policy-making processes with an analysis of the nature of urban policy problems to illuminate the fundamental relationships between the structure of the city's governmental institutions and the process of urban problem solving. Both parts of the analysis take considerable space because both deal with intricate subjects.

The point of this approach is to make political analysis serve as a useful foundation for the analysis of policy problems and vice versa. I have long felt that the application of political analysis to public policy problems has suffered from two serious limitations. Either public policy analysis is primarily an analysis of governmental institutions with public policy language tacked on to suggest a concern for what the institutions actually do. Or it tends to be a straightforward analysis of different ways to solve a policy problem with little concern for the government structures out of which problems arise and which must be relied upon to implement the problem-solving strategy turned up by policy analysis.

The premise of this book is that we cannot understand the failure of urban problem solving without a clear understanding of the way that the urban policy-making system works. Indeed that system constitutes a great part of the original problem. At the same time we cannot understand the character of the urban policy-making system without seeing how it is currently shaped by the nature of the problems it is trying to deal with and how it has evolved over time in response to the need to deal with a variety of different historical problems.

There are three further points that I wish to make at the outset about the character of my argument. First, I seek to explore both the political and administrative sides of urban government and, in particular, to focus on the politics of urban administration as it is expressed in the delivery of urban services. This focus is worth noting only because so much of urban analysis has proceeded on the basis of an analytical separation of urban politics and administration (or management). Until quite recently the available books on urban government dealt with urban administration—treatises on new techniques in urban management and strategies for increasing administrative efficiency. From a political point of view these books were arid; politics was something to be avoided in the name of municipal progress. From any point of view the classic texts on municipal administration failed to convey a vivid sense of the daily practice and perplexity of urban policy making.

Reacting against this tradition, Edward Banfield and James Wilson designed their influential book, *City Politics*, as a "political approach" to urban government.[2] Their approach led them to examine the roles of various political actors and interests in the city and to stress their strategies and behavior and the cleavages between them. In moving urban political analysis away from administrative principles and toward political behavior, Banfield and Wilson made the important contribution of making city politics appear to be a lively part of the American political system. But in so doing, they blurred the question of whether the urban system is distinctive—different in its political behavior and processes from other American governmental institutions. Curiously the earlier writers had at least underlined the special character of city government by emphasizing the city's distinctive functions—sanitation, police administration, and the like.

My hope in this book is to unite the political and administrative understanding of city government in a way that both demonstrates the distinctiveness of the city as an administrative system and

sheds light on the causes and consequences of pluralist democracy in the American system. We cannot understand urban politics without understanding the character of urban service delivery.
And we cannot understand the problems involved in the governance and control of urban services without understanding the extreme pluralism of urban politics. In this sense the "political" and
the "administrative" are inevitably conjoined.

Second, this book draws heavily on the experience of New York
City and New Haven in the last two decades. Both cities have been
at the forefront of efforts to deal with urban problems, and both
have attracted a disporportionate share of attention from urban
scholars and policy analysts. If one draws on historical accounts of
urban problems and policy making, as I have done heavily in this
book, one finds that to an extraordinary extent one is constantly
reading the history of New York City.

This book is also based to a large extent, and in ways that are not
always evident, on my own personal experience in urban government. Different writers get their ideas and understandings in different ways. I know that I could not have written this book if I had
not had the opportunity to observe at first hand the workings of the
mayor's office in New York and New Haven, the office of Neighborhood Government in New York, the New York-Rand Institute,
and the Connecticut Department of Community Affairs. It is because of this experience that I was drawn to examine and analyze
what urban government looks like to the central policy makers in
city hall. It is this experience that has given me whatever "feel" I
may have for the internal workings of city government. Had I
worked with the government of Detroit, Chicago, or Cleveland,
my views of the ungovernable city might be somewhat different,
but I do not think so. I believe that personal experience in government has value only if the interior perspective provides an organizing conception and synthesis of the interacting political forces and
governmental features that are described with great care in the
scholarly literature.

As a scholar, citizen, and sometime participant in urban government, I take no pleasure at all in making the pessimistic argument
that the American city is fundamentally ungovernable in its present
form. For all concerned, I wish that cities were easier to govern.

But I believe that we will never find durable solutions to urban
problems if we do not take a hard and unflattering look at the present incapacity of urban government as a policy-making system. At
this point in American urban history, surely only a compulsive opti-
mist could overlook the distress signals emanating from city hall,
which strongly suggest that the city has become the sick man of
American government.

Acknowledgments

A book that takes four years to write needs a lot of support and assistance, and so it is with this enterprise. In order not to lose the reader before I begin, I will compress my debts, which exist in great magnitude and to many people.

Some people have read all or part of this manuscript and have improved it greatly in doing so. Others have shared their experiences in urban government to my great profit. Among the former are the editors of this series, Jeffrey Pressman and Martha Weinberg, as well as Herbert Kaufman, James Fesler, Donald Kettl, Ira Katznelson, Richard Nelson, and Seymour Sarason. In this regard I owe a special debt to my colleague Ned Woodhouse, who gave an early draft an extraordinarily careful reading and who caused me to bend repeatedly in the face of convincing arguments.

Among those who practice or have recently practiced urban government, I am particularly indebted, for my education and experience, to Robert Sweet, Fred Hayes, Lewis Feldstein, John Lindsay, Richard Lee, and Roy Jones. In the category of both academic and practical experience, I owe great debts to Robert Yin and Peter Szanton of the New York City-Rand Institute, an enterprise without parallel in my experience.

At Yale, I owe institutional debts to John Miller, Charles E. Lindblom, and William Donaldson for support, encouragement, and friendship and to Albert Reiss and Guy Orcutt for a grant to pursue this research.

The development of my argument has also profited from discussions with other colleagues at Yale, especially David Mayhew, Edward Pauly, and Tappan Wilder.

I wish to acknowledge the help of several able people who helped me research and prepare this manuscript: Karyl Hall, Anita Miller, Sam Tomlin, Marie Avitable, and Marya Holcombe.

I am also grateful to various students and urban policy makers who have suffered through earlier versions, both Yale students and various groups of public officials in Connecticut, Missouri, and New York. In the same sense I am grateful to Frank Logue, now mayor of New Haven, and to his legions of National Urban Fellows for experienced observations on the issues I have tried to raise.

Finally there are the debts closer to home. First to James Fesler, to whom this book is dedicated. I do not know a wiser teacher and colleague. And to my wife and son who suffered in various degrees of silence, more the former than the latter, when the other member of the family was doing something else.

The Ungovernable City

1
The Failure of Urban Problem Solving

In the 1960s urban problems gained a special place on the American public agenda. The city was said to be in crisis and urban problems were considered by many to be the most critical problems of American society.

On 15 August 1966, Senator Abraham Ribicoff launched a Senate inquiry into the state of urban government with these words: "the crisis of our cities is the crisis of the modern United States. Seventy percent of all Americans now live in or close to cities. The number grows each year. So the fate of the city and the future of our country are one and the same thing."[1] Speaking on the same day, Senator Robert Kennedy added that "the [urban] problem is the largest we have ever known. And we confront an urban wilderness more formidable and resistant and in some ways more frightening than the wilderness faced by the pilgrims or the pioneers."[2] These words set the tone. The rhetoric of crisis and concern filled the Senate chamber where the Ribicoff subcommittee was meeting for thirty-three days, and it filled 4,437 pages in twenty volumes.[3]

The background of the urban crisis is by now familiar. Michael Harrington's widely read book *The Other America* focused new attention on city slums and their impoverished inhabitants.[4] The civil-rights movement heightened concern for the black urban poor, and widespread rioting and racial conflict deepened the sense of urban crisis.[5]

In response to these events, governments at all levels developed a great number of new urban programs and policies. The federal government led the way. In the war on poverty and later in the model cities program, the Johnson administration fired program after program at the elusive problems of urban education, housing, health, and community development.[6]

One result of this federal activity was a sharp rise in public expenditures for urban programs. Between 1965 and 1972 federal spending for education and manpower, housing, health, and welfare increased almost six times.[7] City budgets showed equally sharp increases.[8] In New York City the expense budget rose from $3.4 billion in 1964–65 to $9.1 billion in 1971–72. Nor, despite popular mythology, was New York an unusually prodigal urban child. In Seattle the expense budget rose from $36.3 million in 1960 to $80.9 million in 1970. In Philadelphia the dollar increase in the expense budget was from $202.3 million in 1960 to $446.3 million in 1971. And in Los Angeles the expense budget leaped from $116.4 million in 1960 to $353.5 million in 1970.

Put in more general terms, the five cities with a 1960 population of a million or more on average increased their spending levels from $148.66 per capita in 1960 to $410.04 per capita in 1970. The seventeen cities with a 1960 population of between 500,000 and a million had an average spending increase from $111.28 per capita in 1960 to $240.01 in 1970. And the twenty-one cities with a 1960 population between 300,000 and 500,000 increased their average spending from $80.45 per capita in 1960 to $178.33 in 1970.

Although New York City was the biggest spender, with a threefold increase in per capita spending during the 1960s, the forty-two next largest cities were not far behind. The twenty-one other cities with 500,000 or more in population increased their spending on average almost two and a half times, and the twenty-one cities with a population of between 300,000 and 500,000 more than doubled their per capita spending in the 1960s.

Despite the proliferation of programs and expenditures, solutions to urban problems were not forthcoming. Within five years of their inception urban problem-solving strategies were increasingly viewed as ineffective or misguided. Many conservatives believed that public money had been wastefully spent. Liberals and radicals often said that not enough money had been spent. Both agreed that urban problems had hardly been dented by the new public programs.

Within five years the brief era of innovation and experimentation in urban problem solving had come to an end, leaving the wreckage of many hopeful programs and policies. But what caused the wreckage? Why were city governments from New York to Los Angeles so unsuccessful in their efforts to solve the urban crisis? Why did so many programs, policies, and attempts to restructure city government prove so disappointing that they were gradually terminated or replaced by yet another batch of hopeful solutions? Why were the infusions of new ideas, resources, and personnel so clearly inadequate to the task of improving the governance of cities?

Very different answers have been given to these questions. One answer is that the war on poverty was a "phony war" fought with totally inadequate resources. Another is that public concern with urban problems dissipated in the face of other crises—Vietnam, the environment, energy, and Watergate. A third, iconoclastic answer offered by Edward Banfield in *The Unheavenly City* is that, given the incorrigible behavior of the lower-class urban poor, it is virtually impossible to improve urban conditions through public policy, however creative.[9]

Whatever the failure of previous urban solutions, the problems that they addressed are still present. The urban crisis may have faded from public attention, but it is alive on the streets and in the neighborhoods of American cities. Urban problems have the distinctive characteristic of being persistent, ordinary, and seemingly intractable.

In 1975 a survey of mayors turned up bleak appraisals of the state of the city. According to Mayor Kenneth Gibson of Newark, "Unfortunately, due to inflation, recession/depression, cutbacks in anticipated State aid to education, shrinking revenues and a general rise in cost of government, we have had to limit services to the point of absolute need."[10] And Mayor Lawrence Cohen of St. Paul, Minnesota, had this to say: "Like most major American cities, St. Paul can no longer finance the ever-increasing cost of essential municipal services with already overstrained . . . revenue sources. In Minnesota, we call it municipal overburden."[11]

A recent study concerned with urban fiscal problems asks, "Can cities survive?"[12] Many cities are laying off policemen and teachers, and prophecies of municipal bankruptcy are no longer merely rhetorical. The experience of New York City makes that plain.

Faced with this frustrating experience, urban policy analysts and students of urban government must carefully reconsider the way they think about urban problems and policies. The question is: How can we best analyze urban problems?

One response, which no longer seems useful, is to recite the litany of urban crisis—to document once more the dimensions of poverty, crime, and housing deterioration and then lament the failures of policemen, teachers, and other urban administrators in dealing with these problems. Another response, which reflects the frustration of many urban activists, is to conclude that in a society characterized by racism, or income inequality, or for that matter by an "unresponsive" federal government, nothing much can be done about urban policy problems. If urban policy making is decisively *determined* by these larger, national forces, the urban poor will stay poor and powerless—unless, of course, the system is drastically transformed. If this view is correct, the city is an irrelevancy, which makes it pointless to talk about urban policy making. However it is impossible to confirm or disconfirm this thesis here. We can only acknowledge it and its significance and move on. A third strategy is that of the policy analyst who searches for immediate answers to particular urban problems. Here the attempt is made to determine whether a particular welfare, housing, or education policy is more effective and less costly than some alternative policy. This is the strategy followed by many economists and systems analysts, program budgeters, and other practitioners of "rational analysis" who gained prominence throughout the government (and in some cities) in the 1960s.[13]

This book follows a very different strategy. Its subject is urban government. Its premise is that the failure of urban problem solving can be found in the nature and structure of city government. It is perhaps not surprising that a political scientist should look for his answers in familiar turf, the structure and working of government. But there are also less subjective reasons for examining urban problem solving through the prism of city government.

It is city government that manages police work and classroom teaching. It is city hall, along with its police, fire, and sanitation employees, that implements social policies and delivers concrete services. It is the job of city government to deal directly with citizens on a daily basis. City employees are the foot soldiers of American government; some would say they are the "dirty workers." Any education policy designed in Washington, D.C., depends heavily on the behavior of particular teachers in particular urban classrooms. A new criminal justice policy will have an impact at the street level (where crimes occur) only if it effectively manages to regulate or change the conduct of individual policemen.

This book makes a simple argument: given its present political organization and decision-making processes, the city is fundamentally ungovernable. By ungovernable I mean that the urban policy-making system is incapable of producing coherent decisions, developing effective policies, or implementing state or federal programs. This means that even if the state or the federal government were to commit large-scale fiscal resources—as they did in the 1960s—it is unlikely that the funds would solve urban problems. It is likely, by contrast, that the policies and programs devised by higher-level government would either never reach their targets at the street level or that they would be completely twisted out of shape or splintered by the time they reached the citizens for whom they were designed.

The implications of this assertion are very serious. If city government provides the foundations for American social policy and if those foundations are shaky (or perhaps crumbling), then the prospects for national programs and policies cannot be very bright. According to this view city government is out of control because it lacks control in its policy making and administration. It is like a ship without a rudder, or perhaps with a hundred rudders pushing it in different directions.

To say that the city is ungovernable is a strong and possibly even a rash claim. It is not a new one. For example, in 1888 James Bryce wrote that "there is no denying that the government of the cities is the one conspicuous failure of the United States."[14] However, it is certainly a debatable claim, and one that can be easily misunderstood. It is therefore crucial to make clear at the outset what I mean and do not mean in saying that the city is ungovernable. I do not mean to say that the problem of urban government is primarily one of evil, stupid, or corrupt political leadership. This may have been true once in some cities, but the days of Boss Tweed, Frank Hague, and other old-style machine pirates are generally over.[15] Chicago has been run by a stubborn, old-fashioned machine, but whatever the exact character of Richard Daley's regime, its notoriety clearly springs from the fact that it is so rare. More important, I am emphatically not saying that the city is ungovernable primarily because it does not have enough money or has too many poor people. Life in urban America would certainly be more pleasant if both the city and its citizens had far greater economic resources; but the lack of money is not, in my view, what prevents city government from governing effectively.

The Central Argument

There is no profit in trying to pin the blame for the city's problems on a scapegoat: the "disorganized" poor or the "racists" in working-class neighborhoods or the bankers or the universities or the public service unions or the brutal policemen. Rather the incapacity of urban government is a product of the city's basic political and social organization and of the nature of the services that it provides.

I do not seek to apologize for or vilify urban policy makers. I wish to explain why city policy makers have been unable to govern effectively. I do not believe that city government is hopeless, but I will not offer instant, miracle solutions either. More precisely, in saying that the city is ungovernable I mean to say that

- the city is too decentralized to permit coherent planning and policy making;
- it is too centralized to support a responsive, flexible relationship between what Albert Reiss calls "the servers and the served in service delivery;"[16]
- it is too dependent on higher-level governments to take strong, independent policy initiatives; and
- it is too independent of higher-level government to ensure competence, control, and fairness in the implementation of national programs.

Viewed in another light, the city can be said to be ungovernable because the principal actors in it have so little control over its governance. That is,

- to a large extent the mayor does not control his bureaucracies and administrators;
- to a large extent high-level administrators do not control their street-level bureaucrats: the teachers, firemen, and policemen who deliver services at the street level;[17] and

• citizens and citizen groups have little control over policy making, however strong and frequent their demands. Additionally citizens find that participation in urban policy making carries high costs and elusive benefits.

Finally, the city can be said to be ungovernable because

• Its problems arise from the city's special function: direct, personal service delivery at the street level—when street-level service delivery issues involve trust, responsiveness, and authority relations between the servers and the served. Thus service problems involve intricately related social, psychological, and political components. They are not simply economic problems that can be solved by the efficient allocation of greater fiscal resources.

• Some of the city's problems are impossible to avoid and solve as long as the city performs its historical function of absorbing the newest, poorest immigrants and managing the ensuing community conflict among different groups in a melting pot that, as Daniel Moynihan and Nathan Glazer have argued, does not melt.[18]

• No city government has ever figured out how to solve some of its enduring policy problems. We do not know how to stop street crime or drug addiction or how to improve the reading levels of low-income children.

The Urban Jigsaw Puzzle: The Problem of Fragmentation

To suggest that the city is ungovernable for these reasons is only to offer a description of the major obstacles to successful urban policy making. It is more important to ask why these obstacles arise. Why is urban government a jigsaw puzzle that few people ever seem able to put together? What we need is a persuasive explanation of why urban management and policy making are such a frustrating business.

City government is an intractable jigsaw puzzle because of the inherent fragmentation of urban service delivery and the historical fragmentation of urban policy-making processes. At first glance this explanation may seem familiar, even obvious; urban observers have been talking about the fragmentation of the city for a long time. To take only one example, Robert Fogelson called his study of Los Angeles *Fragmented Metropolis*,[19] and urban politicians of all stripes, from reformers to machine bosses, have struggled to bring political or managerial order to the fragmented city. So there can be no claim to the notion of originality in the simple mention of fragmentation. However, what has been lacking in urban analysis, political or otherwise, is a systematic examination of the sources, manifestations, and implications of urban fragmentation.

What I hope to do is to demonstrate the explanatory power of the concept of fragmentation when it is broken down into its many different but interacting elements. I will do this not by describing the formal structure of urban government but by looking at the city as a policy-making system, as a complex organization trying to solve particular problems. This involves an attempt to look inside the "black box" of urban policy making to see how problems arise from the street level and how they are channeled and dealt with in the city's decision-making networks. In particular this approach involves studying the policy-making process from the perspective of different political actors—mayors, top-level administrators, street-level bureaucrats, businessmen, neighborhood groups, public unions. Thus I seek to present an interior view of urban policy making by portraying the choices and dilemmas that political participants face. In this sense my argument builds on Wallace Sayre and Herbert Kaufman's *Governing New York City*.[20] Sayre and Kaufman argued that urban politics is best viewed as a struggle between many different contestants for the "stakes of the game." But what kind of struggle, and how are the contestants armed? And how is the nature of the struggle and the contestants' strategies shaped by the defining characteristics of urban politics? In another well-known study Norton Long describes local politics as an "ecology of games."[21] This is true as far as it goes. But what are the different "ecologies" of urban government, and how are the various games played in the urban policy-making process?

In recent political analysis the black box of urban policy making has been left unopened. Lately, to be sure, there has been much discussion of public policy, policy making, and decision making, but the meaning and significance of a public policy approach has not been clearly stated.

Does focus on the policy-making process amount to anything? I believe it does. It means that decision processes explain in important ways the outcomes of decision. Political analysts have long looked to the idea of process as a powerful way of explaining the workings of government. But they have not always underscored the theoretical reason for dwelling on process. That reason must be that the form of policy making decisively shapes the content of policy outcomes. Translated into the urban context, this means that urban policy is unresponsive, unstable, erratic, severely fragmented, and often ineffectual because policy making has these same characteristics. To put it in the simplest possible terms, policy cannot be effective policy without effective policy decisions.

Taking a policy-making approach to urban government leads to two sorts of questions. First are questions about the processes of policy making. How do citizens express their demands for urban services and to whom? How are these demands aggregated (if at all)? What kind of communication exists between those who receive services and those who deliver them? How does the agenda of urban problem solving get set? How stable or unstable is the network of decision making and the configuration of decision makers? Are decisions made at any point, or do they bounce about continuously from decision point to decision point? Once a decision is made, how many decision points are there in the process of implementation? In calling the city ungovernable I am saying that the city's decision routes constitute a maze, and an unstable one at that.

Second are questions about the substance of the policy-making process—questions about the nature of urban problems and the way problems and policies travel along the city's decision networks. How rapidly are problems and demands generated? How does the "clearance rate" for existing problems compare with the entry rate for new problems? Are the demands and problems varied or recurrent, predictable or erratic? Are problem situations clearly defined or highly ambiguous? Is the decision-making process itself coherent or fragmented?

These are the kinds of questions that I believe must be explored if we wish to understand how urban policy making operates. In many cases the questions may seem routine and the answers obvious. But these are not the questions that have motivated and guided urban political analysis in the last generation.

Beyond Community Power

For almost two decades urban political analysis has been dominated by the community power debate. The central question in the debate is: Who governs[22] the city? Is it a power elite in corporate boardrooms or an executive-centered coalition[23] in city hall, or warring sovereignties,[24] or political machines or public unions, or possibly even organized crime? Academic detectives have shown an almost insatiable appetite for finding new and seemingly better answers to this mystery. Nevertheless two main positions persist. One is the power elite conception originally associated with Floyd Hunter's study of Atlanta.[25] The other is the pluralist conception originally associated with Robert Dahl's study of New Haven. In the wake of these studies political analysts have devoted enormous time and energy to the task of appraising and defining the arguments made by the power elite and pluralist schools. Without question the community power debate has made an important contribution in stimulating urban analysis, but the concerns of the debate are not ours here.

I will avoid the community power controversy for two main reasons. First, both sides of the debate are obsessed with the distribution of power and seem to assume that there is a simple relationship between the distribution of power and the process of decision making. By contrast my concern is with how different policy-making processes channel and constrain the exercise of power. Thus, to say that x holds y amount of power is not to give an adequate account of how he uses or fails to use that power to influence or control a particular decision. More precisely I will show that given the complexity of decision routes and networks and the great diversity of decision contexts, the exercise of power is a complicated transaction involving many different political resources and strategies, and various constraints and costs. Power is not mechanically related to policy making. To exercise power is not merely to press a button and make a decision happen. Lying between power and decision, and defining their relationship, are the intricate routes and networks of the policy-making process.

The mechanical, self-actuating view of power is close to what Floyd Hunter is talking about in *Community Political Structure*.[26] His power elite is able to get what it wants. If it could not, it would not be a power elite. If we had good reason to believe that the power elite view accurately characterized urban government in most of our large cities, my emphasis on the urban policy-making process would be unjustified. It would only be complicating a simple matter. As it turns out, however, strong evidence to support the conception that a city is controlled by a command-giving power elite simply has not emerged.

A second reason why I will avoid the community power debate is that most of the analysis that it has produced presents a static picture of urban politics. Both power elite and pluralist theorists leave us with a single, fixed taxonomy of power and decision making. A power elite is a power elite. That is all we need to know if our concern is to describe power relations and, by inference, the structure and health of democratic government. But it is not enough if we are concerned with urban problem solving—with the way urban government responds to different pressures and problems. It is hard to believe that knowing whether a city government has a pluralist or elitist power structure tells us much, if anything, about the way the government deals with busing conflicts, union strikes, street crime, health service delivery, and garbage collection. Community power analysis may show who is instrumental in making decisions but not how they make decisions, what decisions they make, and how effective (or ineffective) their decisions are in dealing with different urban problems.

Comparative Urban Politics

Another important strand of urban political research in recent years has focused on the comparative analysis of American cities. Various writings have tried to categorize and classify different urban political structures and policy-making processes.[27] There are accounts of "caretaker" governments,[28] "amenity producing" governments,[29] and "fused polylithic" governments.[30] In addition studies of urban politics have traditionally emphasized the differences between mayor-council and city-manager forms of government, strong mayor and weak mayor forms, and machine and reform governments.[31]

The trouble with the comparative approach is that for all the differences and similarities it uncovers, it tells little about the basic character of urban government. We want to know here what is distinctive about the urban policy-making process. And to do this, we need to compare the urban system with other kinds of policy-making systems; the obvious point of comparison is with state and national governments.

Urban Systems Analysis: The Inputs and Outputs of City Government

There is yet another mode of analyzing city (and state) government that has recently achieved prominence but that also pays very little attention to what is inside the black box of urban policy making. This approach is usually called systems analysis and draws on David Easton's conception of the "political system."[32] In the system's framework inputs of various sorts go into a black box (which is the policy-making process) and outputs in the form of policies, and expenditures (in general, "authoritative allocations") come out. Applied to state and local governments, this approach has generated many elaborate statistical studies of (1) how socioeconomic differences affect government policies (on the input side) and (2) how governments spend their money and how expenditures differ, between programs and over time (on the output side). The intent of these analyses is to relate input to output and thus to explain why government produces what it does.

Unfortunately analysis of this sort tends to beg basic questions about how urban governments go about making policy choices. Thomas Dye, for example, assesses the primacy of socioeconomic conditions in state government and has no compelling reason to look into the policy-making process.[33] His argument is that the significant differences between Mississippi and New York are economic and that policy making is an epiphenomenon that is controlled by the state's socioeconomic environment. Other writers, most notably J. Patrick Crecine, pay meticulous attention to the pattern of budget expenditures in urban governments.[34] But, like Dye, Crecine presents a deterministic model that makes urban policy making a relatively mechanical operation. Dye's determinism is straightforward; he asserts that economic factors largely determine governmental policy making. Crecine's determinism is more subtle. It results from defining urban policy outputs in terms of budgetary expenditures. In Crecine's view one understands urban policy making by seeing what government spends its money on and how much it spends. At first glance this does not seem to be an unreasonable approach; government budgets obviously reveal a great deal about what a government is doing in its programs and policies. They not only capture the range of government activities, they also capture the relative allocation of financial resources between departments or programs and, with that, the development and decline of particular programs.

However, the budget provides only an introduction to urban policy analysis. All it tells about government activities is that there are large and critically important areas of urban policy making that it does not illuminate at all. In the first place, the fact that a government spends x amount of money in a department often does not reveal the nature or meaning of programs that the department is, in fact, running. A police department may spend x amount on (1) new plainclothes detectives (designed to reduce street crime), or (2) new traffic cops, or (3) new shoe-fly investigators (designed to reduce corruption in the department). The policy significance of the three expenditures would obviously vary considerably, but, as long as the amounts are the same, the choice of one policy will look the same as any other in aggregate budget expenditures.

Urban Policy Making: An Overview

I have spent considerable time appraising existing approaches to urban policy making to show both the limitations of these approaches and the important questions that they ignore. What is my approach? I have said that I will emphasize the process by which decisions are made and that, more precisely, policy-making processes powerfully determine the substance of policy. But what determines the nature of urban policy making? The answer is found in the structure of urban government, which is defined by the central process of city government: the demand for a supply of urban services.

I will show in chapter 2 that this structure is deeply fragmented because of the character of urban services. The argument of this book is thus anchored in a *structural* analysis of what makes the city a distinctive political system, indeed, an intractable political jigsaw puzzle. However, it is not enough to describe the structural foundations of urban policy making. We also want to know what problems city government faces and how it goes about dealing with them. To do this, we need first to analyze the character of urban problems. In doing so, we must avoid the familiar trap of seeing only the present conditions. The failing of much of the urban crisis literature is that it does not distinguish between the capacities of city hall to solve different problems and it gives no historical perspective on urban problem solving. By contrast, how has the problem-solving capacity of urban government developed? What has the city successfully dealt with? What problems have constantly eluded it?

What accounts for the differential performance in problem solving? In chapter 3, I will present a developmental analysis of how urban government has evolved as urban policy makers faced different problems and sought to establish an effective system of governance.

Having examined the structure of urban government and the nature of urban problems, I am in a position to analyze the structure of urban policy making. In chapter 4, I consider what the policy-making and problem-solving process looks like to a central policy maker in city hall. I postulate the existence of a central policy maker who has to sort out and respond to the full range of urban demands and problems. This hypothetical policy maker bears some resemblance to the mayor of a large city, but he is not exactly like a mayor, for he is able to see the workings of the entire policy-making, problem-solving system, and, of course, no actual urban decision maker has this kind of overview. (Many problems and decisions simply do not reach the mayor.) What is involved is the construction of an analytical model of problem generation and agenda setting in the city. The point of the model is to emphasize the uncertainty and instability of urban policy making. Because problems and demands come into the urban policy-making system in an almost infinite number of permutations and combinations, there can be no such thing as one simple model of urban decision making. Urban policy problems differ according to the nature of the problem, the issue context, the stage of decision, the configuration of participants, the institutional setting, and the governmental function involved.

I am concerned with urban government as a policy-making system, and thus with the kinds of problems a policy maker faces and the way he reacts to them. The crux of the argument is that urban policy making is itself fragmented and unstable. Most especially, it is reactive; urban policy makers are constantly rushing from one small crisis to another. In their reactivism they bounce from one hopeful policy response to another, constantly remake and undo decisions, and often search blindly for some solution that will work. Thus a central argument of this book is that the urban policy-making system, because of its reactivism and instability, is different from other policy-making systems, and this difference springs from the fragmented structure of urban government and from the nature of the policy problems that city governments must deal with. In chapter 5, I will move beyond an analysis of the variability and instability of urban policy making to show what makes some urban issues more difficult than others and others almost impossible to manage. In this analysis I again take the perspective of the central policy maker and attempt to illuminate the central elements that distinguish relatively easy problems from hard and virtually intractable ones.

Having constructed a conceptual model of the city's policy-making process, I will examine the way different political actors operate in and react to the policy-making process. What are the political resources and strategies that mayors employ in trying to shape urban policy? What are the constraints and costs that they face? These questions concern the political economy of involvement in policy making for different actors, and they are obviously central to understanding who wins and who loses how much on what kinds of urban policy issues. In chapter 6, I will thus analyze the incentives and obstacles that mayors face and will try to show that the strategy of influence that any particular mayor employs depends on subtle features of issue context, political style, and institutional setting. In the final chapter I will examine the future of the ungovernable city and appraise a number of prominent strategies for solving its problems. I will not however offer any simple solutions to the enduring problem of urban governance.

2
What Makes City Government Different?

The city has a distinctive political and governmental system—a system that deals with policy problems in a particular way and that is greatly limited in its policy-making capacities. In making this argument, it is important not to claim too much. It is obvious, for example, that in any national political system the city is to some extent the creature of larger social and economic forces and is also to some extent a dependent subunit directly controlled by higher-level governments. For example, mayors frequently blame their problems on the economy, white suburbs, or the federal government. In fact, to the extent that the problems of the urban black poor are directly connected to problems in the social and economic structure of the rural South, we would be mistaken to view the urban racial problem as a particular urban problem in isolation from more general patterns of American race relations.

No urban system stands in complete isolation from or is completely independent of the larger society and political system that it inhabits. In the political systems of England, France, Sweden, and the Soviet Union, the city, very much an administrative subunit of the national government, plays only a small and highly dependent role in the formation and implementation of social policy.[1]

By contrast, in the American federal system national government has never had comparable control over or domination of the urban polity. Although cities have a growing financial dependence on higher-level governments, city governments retain substantial independence.[2] Urban policy makers still establish the basic character of policy and administration in their schools, police departments, sanitation departments, housing authorities, redevelopment agencies, and planning departments. Urban officials may not be able to replace their slum housing with handsome new housing projects because they lack the money to do so. But if the federal government had the money for such projects and the city did not want to build them, the new projects would not be built, at least not within city limits. As Martha Derthick has vividly shown, this is exactly what Lyndon Johnson discovered when he tried to get city governments to agree to federal plans for "new towns-in-town" (to be built on federally owned land within city limits).[3]

The stubborn independence of urban policy making de~' from the historical decentralization of the American poli*' tem, from the weakness of state governments in controlling their cities, and from the legal doctrine of home rule, which confers independent authority on city government.

Having argued the point that urban governments are not mere puppets of higher-level governments, we can return to our original question. What are the distinguishing features of city government and how do these features determine the success (or failure) of urban policy making?

It would take another full-length book to do even rough justice to those questions. So I offer the following "distinctive" characteristics of the urban system briefly and schematically as assumptions on which my model of urban policy making is built. By distinctive characteristics I mean that the urban system either possesses the relevant characteristic and other levels of government lack it completely, or, in a somewhat weaker sense, that the characteristic is far more strongly manifest in the urban system than elsewhere. The argument is that the differences between the city system and other systems on the following eleven characteristics, taken together, constitute a fundamental difference that justifies calling the urban system distinctive.

1. *Urban government is a service delivery system* The basic function of urban government is service delivery, and urban service delivery is a distinctive function. Urban services are daily, direct, and locality specific. Fire and police protection, garbage collection, and public education are delivered to particular people in particular neighborhoods on a regular basis. With many of these ordinary urban functions, citizens can immediately tell whether a service has been delivered: they can see whether the trash has been picked up or whether the pothole, broken traffic light, or ruptured water main has been fixed. In these cases urban services are also distinctly tangible and visible. This point is borne out by table 1, a survey of leading complaints about urban services or complaints, which emphasize the daily, even ordinary, character of urban service delivery.

Urban policy making grows up from the street, and it is the street-level service relationship between citizens and public employees that makes city government distinctive. As one student of

Table 1

Rank	Complaint	Mayors	Councilmen
1	Dog and other pet control problems	60.7	44.3
2	Traffic control (stop signs & lights, parking)	40.7	53.5
3	Rezoning problems	30.1	46.3
4	Potholes in streets	30.6	32.4
5	Tax rates	22.0	26.0
6	Sewer service	23.1	19.3
7	Cleanliness of streets, neighborhoods	18.5	19.7
8	Crime	17.0	14.5
9	Housing	15.4	14.3
10	Other[a]	14.1	15.6
11	Water service	10.6	5.9
12	Drugs	6.2	4.3
13	Health care	3.3	2.1
14	Fire protection	2.9	1.4

Source: "America's Mayors and Councilmen," NLC, 1974, from "Municipal Government Today: Problems and Complaints," Nations Cities (April 1974): 9–11.
a. 158 other frequent citizen complaints also were listed by mayors and city councilmen. Among them police-community relations, 27; lack of recreation facilities, 23; administrative duties, lack of action, 23; youth activities, 17; overall appearance of city, 12; ecology problems, 12; snow removal. 11.

the city observed in 1904, the street is the mainspring of urban government:

The problems of the street are the first, the last, and the greatest of the material problems of the city. It is the street that makes the city possible to begin with, that permits the city's growth year by year, and that finally must check the increase of population and business by sheer inability to provide opportunity for movement. In the street we have the first and the best example of the purpose of city government. Here, by the cooperation of the whole community a free way is provided, an "open road," a channel for traffic and transportation for the use of all alike. It is seldom realized how large a share of municipal activity is carried on in the street. Besides the work of making and improving the street itself; besides the work attendant upon the service of public utilities upon, over, and under the street, we must remember that the police department is mainly a street department [and so is sanitation] and that the fire department is absolutely dependent upon the street for its efficiency.[4]

Significantly there is almost no public debate over the proposition that these basic services should be provided by city government. The familiar adage says that there is no Democratic or Republican way to clean the streets. Unlike their attitudes to many national issues that engender intense debate concerning the programs or policies that should be adopted by government, urban residents and urban officials seem to have a clear understanding of what basic services urban government is supposed to provide.

2. *The service relationship is personal* Urban service delivery often involves a street-level relationship between citizens and public employees that is not only direct but personal. Consider the relationship between citizens and city government in police, education, welfare, and health services. In these arenas the character of service delivery is heavily dependent on the attitudes, values, and behavior of the particular citizen and public employee involved. To this extent urban service delivery tends to be distinctively individualistic, even atomistic. Unlike their bureaucratic counterparts in the departments of state or national government, policemen, teachers, and social workers are often required by the logic of their jobs to become involved directly in the personal lives of their clients. Effective urban service delivery depends ultimately on the establishment of what Albert Reiss calls a "civil relationship"—a

mutually supportive relationship between the servers and the served.[5] It is well known that teachers assume a nearly parental role in working with their students, and policemen and social workers have to deal with all sorts of personal problems and difficult social relationships in the course of their daily work. For policemen the most dramatic example of this facet of service delivery is the task of handling what are politely called domestic disputes—fights between husbands and wives or between parents and children.

There are many other equally sensitive disputes that street-level bureaucrats are called on to deal with: street fights between juvenile gangs or between different ethnic racial groups in a school lunchroom or on a school bus or between friends in a bar. There are others too: a student who persistently disrupts a classroom, a student who is chronically truant, a runaway, a former husband who returns to his family from time to time and insists on being taken in, a son who regularly shows signs of being beaten up by someone, a Saturday night drunk, a former mental patient who occasionally "goes off" and is viewed by neighbors as a "public nuisance." The list is long; some street-level bureaucrats would say endless. The point is that handling the problem requires a direct personal intervention in the life of a family, apartment building, classroom, or block.

3. *The divisibility of urban services* Citizen demands are deeply fragmented because of the nature of urban public services. Because urban services are personalized and locality specific, they are highly divisible, both in terms of delivery and citizen demands.

Unlike pure public goods like national defense or national parks, urban services tend to be highly divisible, in quantity and quality, between different individuals, blocks, or neighborhoods. One of the most familiar citizen complaints in city government is that a particular block or neighborhood is not receiving its fair share of services. Conversely urban administrators can make countless small adjustments and reallocations both in their deployment of street-level bureaucrats and in their definition of what service policies and procedures should be followed in a particular neighborhood. Police administrators may decide to crack down on prostitution or teenage gangs in one area of the city but not in others. School administrators may develop bilingual programs, enrichment programs, or strict disciplinary procedures in certain classrooms and schools but not others.

4. *Variation in need* There is enormous variation in individual needs and demands for city services. Service demands may vary from individual to individual on a block, from block to block, and from neighborhood to neighborhood. They also vary according to the race, economic position, age, sex, and family composition of urban residents.

In the first place neighborhoods differ in their demands for services. A particular neighborhood might be satisfied with police and fire protection but dissatisfied with health and garbage service.[6] Demands by individuals and neighborhoods for a particular service differ both qualitatively and quantitatively. The question is not simply how much police protection but what kind: street patrol, juvenile crime specialists, or decoys seeking to deal with street crime. On garbage collection the question is not only how often and how regular the collection is but also what the mix is between daily pickup, street sweeping, and bulk pickup.

In quantitative terms economic, social, and physical factors (such as population density and age of housing) affect the amount of fire protection and garbage collection demanded in the area. In terms of quality, differences in community structure strongly affect the precise nature of service demands. A low-income neighborhood with a large number of drug addicts will have different demands for police protection than a commercial strip, an entertainment area, or a neighborhood of middle-income homeowners or those with a high proportion of elderly people or college students. Moreover demands for police service may vary dramatically between different groups within such neighborhoods. In low-income, high-crime neighborhoods, for example, older residents will often seek much tougher law enforcement against young delinquents while young residents, who like to hang out, will demand less police surveillance and less law enforcement. In these cases qualitative differences in the demand for services complicate the determination of what kinds of laws should be enforced (or not enforced), what kinds of crime are feared, what time of day that police protection is most needed, and what kind of public place residents wish to maintain.

In addition to neighborhood differences, service demands will often differ on a block-by-block, household, or individual basis. As Gerald Suttles has shown, both blocks and neighborhoods tend to have highly complex "ecologies" and turf.[7] In Suttles's account even a small park may contain a variety of separate conflicting social worlds.

These differences are important because many urban service problems affect a very small public, and the solution of one problem is often entirely independent of the solution of others. The defective traffic light, the broken catch basin, the abandoned car, the after-hours bar, the rubbish fires in a vacant lot, the broken park benches and swings, the noise and fumes from a small factory, and the addict's hangout are all problems that affect a small group of residents intensely and other residents not at all. In short because the delivery of and the demand for urban services is so locality specific, one resident may be satisfied with service delivery while his neighbor is highly discontented. For example, the fact that garbage is collected regularly at one home does not mean that it has been collected down the block or around the corner. More important, it does not matter to an urban resident that urban services are delivered well elsewhere. This gives him no material or symbolic satisfaction. His concern and demand are that services be provided to him, his family, his house, and his block.

Given the number and diversity of cleavages in citizen service demands and given the fact that citizens tend to have a well-crystallized sense of their own service interests (because the services are tangible and visible), the structure of citizen demands for services thus is deeply fragmented.

5. *Urban political organizations* These diverse, fragmented citizen interests have produced a bewildering array of street-level community organizations that seek to give voice to one neighborhood demand or another. Typically they represent highly segmented and crystallized political interests: any neighborhood is likely to have scores of these small, competing community organizations.

At the height of community organization in the late 1960s, many blocks on the Lower East Side of New York City had two or three different community organizations on the same block. In 1970 I counted over two hundred different community organizations in a twenty-square-block area of the Lower East Side. This is not a new phenomenon. According to Sayre and Kaufman, writing more than ten years ago, "No careful census of [these] nongovernmental groups has ever been made, but the number seems to run at least to tens of thousands. This estimate comprises only those groups sufficiently well organized to have letterheads, telephones, and/or to appear in some published directory."[8] Some of these groups are traditional and well known: church associations, neighborhood chambers of commerce, as well as Rotary, Kiwanis, and Lions clubs, PTAs, police precinct councils, NAACP and CORE chapters, ethnic associations (be they Hibernian Societies or Attillean Associations), and neighborhood social clubs ranging from youth gangs to senior citizen centers to the storefront clubhouses where older men congregate in Italian and Spanish neighborhoods. More recently a new generation of neighborhood organizations has grown up and added to the fragmentation of urban politics at the street level. Some of these organizations—community action agencies, neighborhood health councils, and neighborhood service centers—were direct outgrowths of the war on poverty and provided the main impetus behind what Daniel Bell and Virginia Held have called the "community revolution."[9] Bell and Held argue that there may be "more participation than ever before in American society, particularly in the large urban centers such as New York, and more opportunity for the active and interested person to express his political and social concerns."[10] They continue:

Forty years ago, a Tammany political boss could give an order to a mayor. Today, no such simple action is possible. On each political issue—decentralization or community control, the mix of low income and middle income housing, the proportion of blacks in the city colleges, the location of a cross-Manhattan or cross-Brooklyn expressway, etc.—there are dozens of active, vocal, and conflicting organized opinions. The difficulty in governing New York—and many other cities as well—is not the "lack of voice" of individuals in city affairs, or the "eclipse of local community," but the babel of voices and the multiplication of claimants in the widened political arena. In this new participatory democracy the need is for the creation of new political mechanisms that will allow for the establishment of priorities in the city, and for some effective bargaining and tradeoffs between groups; without that the city may end in shambles.[11]

Such organizations as block associations, tenants' councils, neighborhood associations, decentralized school boards, food cooperatives, organizations of welfare mothers, taxpayers' groups, drug prevention groups, citizen street patrols, and protest groups of all shapes and sizes further reflect the participatory mood of the late 1960s.

Not all of these groups still exist; some were in operation for only a few weeks or months; some were never more than paper organizations operating out of the living room of a single neighborhood activist. If it is hard to find out who is in charge in city government, it is that much harder to find the voice of the community in the many voices that rise from it. One thing is clear, however: if policemen, firemen, and teachers are the foot soldiers of city governments, then members of these neighborhood groups are the foot soldiers of the community in dealing with city government. They take the lead in pressing complaints and in fighting city hall. They are the principal neighborhood combatants in the many-sided contest of urban politics.

6. *Political representation in the city* In most large American cities the system of political representation is weakly developed and provides little articulation of citizen interests. City councilmen are typically part-time officials who are underpaid and understaffed and are rarely involved in significant policy making. Exhortations to strengthen the city's representative bodies are by now a familiar element in urban political discourse. As many urban political analysts have noted, councilmen still tend to play a passive role in policy initiation and in the control of urban administration. Charles Adrian makes the point with the following example: "When the bus companies came to the councils from time to time asking for fare increases, each councilman would deplore the trend toward higher fares and poorer service, but since the only discernible alternative to refusing the rate increase was a discontinuance of service, almost all councilmen voted in favor of the request. In each of the cities, study committees of lay citizens were appointed to seek solutions to the bus problem. . . . In each case,

the council gratefully, and with little discussion, accepted the proposed solutions."[12] And a study of California city governments by Betty Zisk concludes that urban representation is a one-way street.[13] Local groups actively press their requests and interests on local representatives, but the representatives do not listen or respond.

Urban political representation is also fragmented by overlapping city, county, state, and national constituencies. Who serves the interests of urban residents and to whom does the urban resident look for help: his councilman, state assemblyman, state senator, congressman, or senator? At one time the great machines provided political linkage between urban representatives. But with the demise of the machines in most cities, urban representatives are now apt to produce rival, and often warring, sovereignties. Further, because of the deep fragmentation of interests in any given neighborhood, it is intrinsically difficult, if not impossible, for any political representative to express the interests of his urban district in a coherent, consistent way. In state legislatures and the Congress representatives are better able to express their district's interest in a generalized way. Indeed state and national policy making often reflects a compromise between relatively well-defined urban interests and rural ones, and the interests of cattle-producing, ship-building, coal-mining, timber-cutting, or textile-milling districts are clearly and forcefully articulated. By contrast there is no comparable specialization of producer interests in urban neighborhoods. Urban politics revolves around consumer interests, which are expressed in citizen demands for urban services, and every neighborhood has similar and equally diverse service demands and interests. As a result of both these factors the task of political representation falls on the many, highly localized neighborhood organizations and, to a very real extent, on the individual residents themselves. Importantly these street-level organizations operate largely outside of formal, political channels. Rather than focusing their energies on general elections or party primaries, they adopt various strategies of direct but informal political action: holding community meetings, protesting, and pressuring street-level bureaucrats and city hall.

7. *Urban politics is bureaucratic politics* Because service delivery lies at the heart of city government and because service delivery

involves at root an ongoing service relationship between citizens and street-level bureaucrats, urban policy making has a distinctively bureaucratic and administrative flavor.

In state and national government where interest groups compete for the dispensations and pork-barrel benefits distributed through legislation, the pressure is strongly focused on the legislature. In urban politics where neighborhood groups are primarily concerned with bureaucratic decision making in regard to the delivery of urban services, the pressure system is focused on urban administrators, beginning with the mayor. The mayor becomes the chief bureaucrat, and city hall becomes the main target of complaints and the crucible of political conflicts. This is a feature of urban policy making that big-city mayors understand very well. According to Mayor Charles Weeler of Kansas City, who has published a diary of life in city hall:

After a day in the mayor's office, I have been amazed at the amount of mail, the number of phone calls, and the multitude of visitors. . . . To me, a city is the most complicated thing in the world. In federal and state government, there is lots of organization—a separation of powers. In a city government there are lots of people, each with a set of interests and some desire to participate. . . . Entering my second full week as mayor of Kansas City, I find it obviously a confusing job. The best word to describe it is mind boggling. Invitations continue to pour in from people who want to see the new mayor. Phone calls and mail continue to descend upon the office.[14]

As Henry Maier, mayor of Milwaukee, once recalled, "At the convivial evening banquet, the Mayor is applauded by the audience. Afterwards, of course, there are those who stop him to lecture and advise, 'Why don't you . . . ? Why haven't you . . . ?' "[15] Stephen Bailey, former mayor of Middletown, Connecticut, once received an angry late-night phone call from a constituent: "Why the hell don't you stop trying to build Radio City and come down here and collect my garbage? It stinks."[16] Carl Stokes vividly described his initiation as mayor of Cleveland: "The trouble with the strong-mayor form of government in a big city is that the mayor is administrator, chief political officer and chief ceremonial officer for the entire city; everything flows to him directly. If he tries to handle all these duties, he becomes immobilized."[17] Finally, consider the mayor's job description as seen by New York City's former mayor, John V. Lindsay:

In some ways, the business of being Mayor of New York City is the most frustrating in the country. His burdens have been described as being second only to that of the President. But a President is recognized as a man with an awesome burden, and many of his most pressing problems are far away from the immediate concerns of the people. But a Mayor is the chief executive of the first line of government. It's his responsibility to see that there are enough police on the streets, modern and sufficient schools, comfortable transportation, heat in the winter, and adequate housing. The things a Mayor does or does not do touch the daily life of people; when his level of government does not work effectively, he feels directly the discontent of his constituency. He also feels it when another level of government does not work effectively.[18]

8. *The role of the mayor* Mayors are distinctive as American political executives because they are in close proximity to their constituents (which makes it easier to fight city hall than the state house or the White House); because they have daily involvement in the administrative details of service delivery; and because the public presumes that the mayor is directly responsible and accountable for street-level service problems. Presidents take credit for their foreign policy accomplishments, and governors may focus on and take credit for their new highways and community colleges. But the people in city hall are the custodians of the sidewalks who must deal every day with the most ordinary and personal needs of their constituents. It is the mayor's job to make an increasingly ungovernable city work.

The first point to be made is that the mayor works in closer physical proximity to his constituents than presidents and governors do. For many urban residents city hall is no farther from their homes than their place of work. Residents can reach city hall or the board of education or the police department by picking up their telephone and making a local call. By contrast the governor's office and the White House are relatively removed in both physical distance and citizen perception.

More important, the mayor is a highly visible political figure. Many urban residents have seen their mayor and spoken with him. He spends a considerable amount of his time out in public—out in the neighborhoods. Fiorello La Guardia of New York City created a small legend for himself by reading the Sunday comics on the radio.[19] Local newspapers often give the impression that the mayor does nothing but attend ground-breaking ceremonies, visit schools and hospitals, review parades, and sit on the dais at the community functions. For this reason and because local government is the least mysterious level of government, the mayor is a more ordinary, less aloof political figure than the governor or the president. The ennobling and highly symbolic aura that surrounds the president and the presidency does not attach to the mayor and the idea of city hall. The president is concerned with the loftiest questions of war and peace and national purpose; the mayor collects the garbage. Thus the man in city hall cannot rely to the same extent on powerful symbols of office to give him a valuable cushion of authority, respect, and deference.

Mayor Maier of Milwaukee made the point in this way: "He [the mayor] thinks of the many different calls upon him for leadership and he recalls how a friend, a former secretary to another may have put it: the great game is to destroy the mayor's authority, prestige, and status and then call upon him for leadership."[20] The mayor is judged by what he does every day, and what he does is deliver services. If service problems exist, as they always will, he is blamed for them as if he were the custodian of drain pipes, potholes, and traffic lights.

We can better understand and explain the role of mayors by considering how the relationship between political leaders and followers differs in urban, state, and national politics. More precisely let us consider two dimensions of the relationship: physical distance between leaders and citizens and the degree of citizen participation in formal political processes.

With the presidency, where the physical distance between leader and citizen is greatest but where citizen participation in elections is also greatest, there is a very strong symbolic link between the president and his constituents. Although the president does not represent many, if any, individual citizens directly, he does represent millions of them in a more abstract, symbolic way. He is the embodiment of a national purpose. As Charles Hardin puts it, "the people cannot govern, and the President has become their surrogate. Accordingly he personifies their political authority. When he speaks *ex cathedra* from atop his pyramid of forty million votes, he is awe-inspiring."[21]

With the governor and state government in general, there is still a great physical distance between leaders and citizens, but citizen participation in elections is greatly reduced. State government has historically had a low salience for most citizens and so has the governor. At the state level citizen demands are carried largely by legislators and interest groups, and their conflicts and compromises take place largely beyond the range of direct citizen demands and political action.

With the mayor the physical proximity between leaders and citizens is greatest, and citizen participation in voting is lowest. The mayor is thus a highly accessible target; citizens expect him to be responsive to their demands. But the formal representation instruments for popular control and accountability are weak. As we have seen, urban neighborhood groups, acting informally, fill this political vacuum.

9. *The mayor and his administration* If the mayor becomes in this way the focal point in the city's fragmented political system, he is not in a structural position to provide coherent policy making and service delivery. In part this is because the mayors of most large cities lack the formal powers to control the administrative system that delivers services to urban residents. His formal power over policy making and service delivery is shared with independent elected officials and with independent or semi-independent departments, boards, and commissions (boards of education, police departments, and city planning commissions). Leonard Ruchelman points out that "in Los Angeles, the mayor shares executive authority with an independently elected city attorney and a comptroller. In addition, nineteen of the twenty-eight city departments are responsible to independent boards and commissions whose members, although appointed by the mayor, can be removed by him only with great difficulty."[22] The following historical account underscores this central point. James Parton discovered that in nineteenth-century New York,

The Mayor has been deprived of all controlling power. The Board of Aldermen, seventeen in number, the Board of twenty-four Councilmen, the twelve Supervisors, the twenty-one members of the Board of Education, are so many independent legislative bodies, elected by the people. The police are governed by four Commissioners, appointed by the Governor for eight years. The charitable and reformatory institutions of the city are in charge of four Commissioners whom the City Comptroller appoints for five years. The Commissioners of the Central Park, eight in number, are appointed by the Governor for five years. Four Commissioners, appointed by the Governor for eight years, manage the Fire Department. There are also five Commissioners of Pilots, two appointed by the Board of Underwriters and three by the Chamber of Commerce. The finances of the city are in charge of the Comptroller, whom the *people* elect for four years. The street department has as its head one Commissioner, who is appointed by the Mayor for two years. Three Commissioners, appointed by the Mayor, manage the Croton Aqueduct department. The law officer of the city, called the Corporation Counsel, is elected by the *people* for three years! Six Commissioners, appointed by the Governor for six years, attend to the emigration from foreign countries. To these has been recently added a Board of health, the members of which are appointed by the Governor.[23]

The mayor also lacks control over urban administration because of that system's fragmentation. Even though many service problems are interrelated, the various service delivery departments tend to function as separate feudal baronies. Mayor Robert Wagner of New York City used to note with pride that he had called his police commissioner on the telephone only a handful of times in the course of an association that lasted several years. This is ostensibly the positive side of feudal politics: professionalism without political influence. But there is clearly a negative side too. After the Watts riots in Los Angeles, Mayor Samuel Yorty was interrogated by a Senate committee about his government's failure to improve urban education in the city. His reply to Senator Ribicoff was this: "I think I must remind you again Senator, I have no jurisdiction whatever over the city schools. . . . Absolutely none, and that is why I tried to make that clear . . . so you would understand . . . how sometimes limited the mayor can be."[24] Or as Mayor John Lindsay once put it: "The bureaucracy has become so big and insensitive. The way these ninety-nine or so agencies are set up, they're often dealing with fractions of problems, fractions that sometimes transcend what the agencies' jurisdictions should be. The system is so damn divisive that its departments have to deal with each other almost by treaty. Imagine three different departments having jurisdiction over paving streets, depending on whether they're in parks or on bridge approaches or in mid-town Manhattan. And does it make any sense to you that sick-baby clinics are under the Department of Hospitals while well-baby clinics are the responsibility of the Department of Health."[25]

In sum when city government tries to gather together the various administrative pieces that control a service delivery sector, it finds a plethora of administrators who have a vested interest and a putative sovereignty over policy making. Again, in Mayor John Lindsay's words: "Stories of conflicts, overlapping jurisdictions, and areas in which no department knew who had jurisdiction were legendary. For example, a complaint about water could be handled by the Buildings Department, the Health Department, or the Department of Water Supply, depending on whether the caller was complaining about no water, insufficient water, or insufficient hot water. Roads could come under the bailiwick of highways, parks, or the Triborough Bridge and Tunnel Authority; indeed, in one case, three different departments were responsible for an eight-mile stretch of road in Queens."[26] As a result of these patterns, any attempt by the mayor to redirect or reorganize service delivery will lead him into complex disputes between administrators over territorial rights and responsibilities and thus into intense bureaucratic conflict.

10. *Vertical fragmentation: The role of street-level bureaucrats*
The fragmentation between urban bureaucracies is compounded in a critically important way by fragmentation in the hierarchical structure of service delivery. Since urban services involve a direct and often personal relationship between public employees and citizens, it is the street-level bureaucrats who must make on-the-spot, personal judgments.

The wide discretion of street-level bureaucrats has frequently been noted, and it is indeed a crucial structural determinant of fragmented service delivery.[27] Although the police commissioner or the school superintendent may try to lay down broad-gauged policies and administrative practices, the foot soldier out on his own on the beat, in the garbage truck, or in the classroom determines to a large extent whether or not central policy is implemented. Even if they were followed, policy directives would lack the subtlety and detail to provide workable operating guidelines for a policeman dealing with an ambiguous or sensitive arrest or a teacher trying to respond to different student needs and problems. Because of the independence and discretion of street-level bureaucrats and the weakness of field supervision, the central administrators in urban bureaucracies have relatively weak control over service delivery at the crucial point of contact between city and citizens.

This means that service delivery takes place in a highly decentralized administrative marketplace, with many different consumers and producers trying independently to strike a bargain on a wide range of goods and services. Lacking workable standards for supplying and evaluating urban services, both citizens and street-level bureaucrats are to a large extent left to their own judgments and to whatever piecemeal accommodations can be worked out between the servers and the served. In this service delivery context of disparate expectations and fuzzy evaluations, service delivery tends to become a series of atomistic encounters between citizens and public employees.

11. *Higher-level governments: federalism and fragmentation* Urban policy making is deeply fragmented by the conflicting authority and policy jurisdictions of national, state, and city governments. Many of the programs and policies of all governments in the American system come to rest—have their direct impact—at the street level. But every level has its claim and source of control in setting urban policy. As a result, urban policy making is often pulled apart from several directions, and there is likely to be frequent conflict and competition between one or more levels of government over the determination of street-level policy.

Urban Fragmentation and Street-Fighting Pluralism

These eleven distinctive characteristics add up to a striking picture of fragmentation in the urban political system, which grows out of the very nature of urban services. It is reinforced by the structure of neighborhood organizations and service bureaucracies, the structure of city government, and the competing policy initiatives and jurisdictions of national, state, and city governments.

These multiple sources of fragmentation might appear at first glance to be just a curiosity of urban governmental and political architecture. Fragmentation might arguably be theoretically uninteresting or unproblematic. Indeed some political analysts, including C. E. Lindblom, argue that political and governmental fragmentation creates the conditions for a political marketplace that allows for "public choice" or disjointed incrementalism—analogues for efficient allocation in economic markets.[28]

My argument is that urban fragmentation does profoundly affect policy making in the city, but not in the benign way Lindblom might suspect. Rather urban policy making takes place in a political and administrative system that is fragmented to the point of chaos. The following description of New York City in 1866 still applies to large U.S. cities: "Perhaps the best way of beginning an investigation of the city government would be to go down to the City Hall and look at it. It proved not to be there. . . . It has been gradually cut to pieces and scattered over the island. . . . Was there such a hodge podge of government before in the world?"[29] There is no coherent administrative order to implement and control public policy. What exists instead is an extreme pluralism of political, administrative, and community interests which produces what I will call "street-fighting pluralism."

Street-fighting pluralism suggests a political free-for-all, a pattern of unstructured, multilateral conflict in which many different combatants fight continuously with one another in a very great number of permutations and combinations. Street-fighting pluralism exists when five different groups in the same neighborhood struggle over policy and expenditures in a local school and when they enlist different city administrators, representatives, or agencies as allies in the fight. It exists when organizations in four different neighborhoods, along with opposed factions in the police department, fight to keep a local police station from being closed down. Or when the mayor, a neighborhood group, and one or more bureaucracies are arguing about an urban renewal project. Or when seven city departments are fighting over a policy that concerns them all. Or when national, state, and local governments are in conflict over the environmental consequences of a sewage treatment plant. The first characteristic of street-fighting pluralism is the diversity of the contestants involved. This diversity of interests begins at the street level, between different people on the same block, between different blocks, between different groups in a neighborhood, and between different neighborhoods. It extends into conflicts between different city bureaucracies, between mayors and bureaucracy, and between city hall and independent boards and commissions. In addition to these "horizontal" dimensions of political interest, there are also vertical dimensions in the diversity of interests that exist between different levels of a bureaucracy and between national, state, and city government. In terms of interest diversity, the urban jigsaw puzzle can be depicted as follows:

White House

HEW   EPA   HUD

State House

State Education   Welfare Housing   Housing Departments

City Hall

Boards   Commissions   Boards   Commissions

City Education   Welfare   Police   Sanitation Departments

Teachers   Social Workers   Policemen   Garbage Men

Neighborhood   Neighborhood   Neighborhood   Neighborhood

Block   Block   Block   Block   Block

Individuals   Individuals   Individuals   Individuals   Individuals

Notice that this is a curious political organization chart, for no lines are drawn between different actors to depict characteristic lines of communication or interaction. This suggests a second central point about street-fighting pluralism: the variability of conflict in city government. With a few exceptions, it is easy to imagine a conflict or a decision game involving any pair or any set of actors. A third characteristic of street-fighting pluralism is the complexity of conflict and decision games, that is, the likelihood is great that urban policy making will involve three, four, five, or ten different individuals and/or institutions.

A fourth characteristic of street-fighting pluralism follows from the diversity, variability, and complexity of urban interests. Urban policy games are unstable, for the players, demands, problems, and conflicts are constantly and rapidly changing. "Fights" break out with different combatants and configurations spasmodically, without any particular pattern or progression.

The fifth characteristic of street-fighting pluralism is that the actors and institutions are highly interdependent—they constantly get in each other's way. The jurisdictions of city, state, and federal governments collide in urban service delivery, and their programs overlap and frequently conflict at the street level. Also the policies and services of police, fire, sanitation, school, and other urban bureaucracies are likely to be interconnected (whether or not they are, in fact, coordinated). Consider the problem of drug addiction in city schools. It concerns police, education, and health bureaucracies, and yet their policies are often separate and disconnected. Or consider the following problems and their involvement of multiple departments: arson, fire and police, street cleaning, sanitation and police; juvenile delinquency, schools, police, and mental health; and family disputes—police and welfare. Finally, urban policy making involves an endless series of tangible trade-offs between individuals, blocks, and neighborhoods.

The sixth characteristic of the city's street-fighting pluralism is that its policy-making games involve direct face-to-face conflict. Unlike the distant relationships between citizens and state government or between citizens and the federal government, urban conflicts mean regular personal encounters between city hall and the neighborhoods.

A seventh characteristic of street-fighting pluralism is that the demands and preferences of urban residents tend to be well crystallized. Urban residents know quite specifically what they want and do not want for their block, school, and parks and what they like and do not like about the services provided by city government. Whereas citizen opinion on national, economic, or foreign policy is likely to be general and vague, citizen opinion about urban services is likely to be narrow and concrete.

In sum, street-fighting pluralism is characterized by the diversity, variability, complexity, instability, and interdependence of interests and decision games and by the fact that policy making involves direct and well-crystallized conflicts about urban goods and services. It is important to note two further points. First, the fact that diverse, variable, and complex interests infuse urban policy making does not mean that each interest has equal power or even substantial power. What is meant is that urban policy makers are faced with, and must react to, a diverse, variable, complex range of demands and that the various urban political actors, whatever their power, must fight it out as best they can. Second, I do not mean to suggest that policy making in state and national government bears no resemblance to urban policy making, or that higher-level governments display none of the defining characteristics of street-fighting pluralism. The argument is that on each dimension of street-fighting pluralism, urban policy making displays a stronger pattern than either the state or national government and that the differences on each dimension add up to a clear structural difference overall.

The Character of Urban Problems

There is no single urban problem; rather there are many different kinds of problems, which have different internal characteristics and require quite different solutions. One way to clarify the nature of urban problems is to ask what it would take to solve them. In recent years one answer has tended to dominate all the others in political discourse. The premise of many federal programs and of many accounts of the urban crisis is that all urban problems require in a solution is money. As John Lindsay put it,

The ultimate problem is money—or, rather, the problem of not enough money. Whatever else a city can do, it cannot provide the services its people want if it does not have the money to pay for them. And we don't have the money. There is no other business I can think of where the proprietor knows absolutely that he will face bankruptcy every year. Yet my own city's expenses—with no increase at all in programs—go up each year three times as much as reserves. That does not make for tranquility. It makes for citizens who must wonder each year whether their local library will cut back its hours, whether their children will be forced to attend split sessions in the schools, and whether their hospital can be modernized to meet inevitably higher demands.[30]

The proposals for a domestic Marshall Plan and for the creation of "federal cities" were similarly based on the assumption that what the city basically needs is more money. In fact, it is plain that many urban problems cannot be approached, much less solved, without a large-scale commitment of new funds. There is no way to build new housing for low-income urban residents without buying bricks, mortar, and the services of the construction trades. It is impossible to construct new highways, public transit systems, hospitals, schools, and parks without substantial capital outlays. Although cities have been able (at least until recently) to undertake significant capital construction every year with the funds derived from municipal bond issues, city halls lack the fiscal resources to develop new housing and adequate schools and parks throughout the city.

If Newark, New Jersey, had an extra billion dollars a year, it would have no difficulty applying it fruitfully to its most pressing problems. But even if Newark had even far greater resources at its disposal, it would quickly find that many of its most critical problems were not amenable to direct fiscal solutions. The city would build many new homes and schools and hospitals; but, having done so, it would still be confronted with the perpetual problems of service delivery. If public employees were thought to be unresponsive, insensitive, arbitrary, and inefficient before the windfall fiscal bonus, it is not clear that hiring more employees would address the core problem. These problems are not fiscal ones to begin with; they are social, political, and administrative ones. More precisely if, as is so often the case, problems arise from the fact that services do not match the needs of residents in a particular area and that citizens lack the information about services and access to those who deliver them, the problem is one of responsiveness in government. The responsiveness problem is also manifest when citizens complain that the city takes too long to respond to their requests or that city administrators stall or evade or get tangled in red tape in the course of dealing with their complaints or requests. The extreme case of the responsiveness problem exists when citizens complain that they cannot get a hearing—that no one in city government will listen to their concerns.

If urban public employees do not follow the policies and procedures designed by city administrators to control and improve service delivery, the problem at the street level is one of regulation,
not of inadequate fiscal resources. If policemen sleep in their cars
or use unnecessary force in dealing with suspects or harass certain
groups of people, the problem is that they are failing to do what
they have been told to do. If sanitation men do not follow their
routes or do not meet their schedule, the problem again is one of
administrative regulation and control. If city health inspectors,
housing inspectors, or building code inspectors fail to report residents' problems or fail to follow up on them, the problem again is
regulation.

If there is deep hostility and little communication between the
servers and the served, the problem is one of trust, not money.
Citizen complaints that public employees are racist, hostile, indifferent, or dishonest reflect a deep lack of trust in the mayor's foot
soldiers. When policemen, firemen, teachers, and social workers
feel that residents do not understand the difficulties of their jobs,
or refuse to cooperate with them, or treat them with disrespect,
the other side of the trust problem in service delivery is manifest.

If the problem is that citizens have no ability to participate in—or
make their preferences known to—government, and if a city government cannot act on a problem like pollution because it does not
control the behavior of adjoining governments, the solution
would appear to lie in a restructuring of government (either
through neighborhood government or metropolitan government). It does not lie in spending more money. Many of the recent
efforts to improve urban policy making have involved restructuring strategies of one sort or another. Community action was an
attempt by the federal government to change the rules of the game
for citizen participation. Model cities was, in large measure, an
effort to create a new planning mechanism for poor neighborhoods. So, too, the various experiments in decentralization and
community control entailed an attempt to restructure political and
administrative power relations between city hall and the neighborhoods. The development of revenue-sharing programs under the
rubric of a new federalism represents yet another attempt to deal

with urban problems by tinkering with the structure of policy making.

Nor are the restructuring strategies something new. The city has been subject to an endless series of restructuring efforts in this century: council-manager government, boards and commissions, independent public authorities, metropolitan government proposals, home rule reforms, and local charter revisions.

In sum, resource problems are important in urban government and especially in the area of physical construction. But in those areas of police, education, health, and social services where the relationship between citizen and public employee is critical, the problem is very likely to be one of responsiveness, trust, or regulation. These problems require subtle political and administrative remedies. Finally, for a growing number of urban issues, including the basic issues of authority and participation between the server and the served, the problem is one of restructuring the rules of the game in city government.

The Character of Urban Policy Making

Urban policy making is an expression of the urban political system —its governmental structure, its social system, and its characteristic problems. Urban policy making is highly fragmented because that is the legacy of its governmental foundations. It is unstable because urban politics and society are unstable. It is erratic and uncertain because so many different problems are constantly arising from the street level, and a large proportion of them escape neat solutions.

Compare this urban world where policy makers are struggling to fix an agenda, sort out issues, and react to myriad problems coming at them directly from the street level with the policy-making environment of state and national government. In state government, where citizens typically do not press specific daily service demands directly on government, the central political interaction is a bargaining process between legislators and organized interest groups.[31] Here the central feature of policy making is political exchange, or logrolling, and compromise. Importantly, this policy-making world is far more self-contained than the world of urban government.

National policy making is still another step removed from the daily articulation of and reaction to diverse neighborhood problems. Although it is undeniably true that congressmen spend a large percentage of their time handling casework for constituents, in their role as policy makers they are far more in control of their agendas and policy-making processes than their urban counterparts.[32] Typically in domestic policy what gets on the public agenda is what congressmen and the president put on it. Congressional policy making is thus characterized by a deliberate (some would say stultifying) process of debate and coalition building in committees, on the floor of the House or Senate, and between the Congress, president, and the bureaucracy. New bills and policies move slowly, if at all, across the procedural hurdles that exist in the highly institutionalized policy-making system of national government.

Few political analysts would claim the national government is too reactive and too unstable in its policy making. The familiar accusation is that the national government is too slow to react to new problems and disturbingly sluggish when it does. Moreover national policy making is rarely characterized by the frantic movement from one problem to another. Instead there is a significant continuity of issues and problems. At any given moment in recent years the president and Congress were likely to be engaged in an ongoing policy discussion or debate about tax policy, military expenditures, health insurance, environmental protection, or compensatory education programs. And not only have policy discussions on these issues been steady, but actual decision making has tended to involve only marginal shifts from prior policy.

In sum, urban policy making is disinctively fragmented, unstable, and reactive. City hall must constantly react to a barrage of particular service problems that arise unpredictably and erratically. It may be forced to worry about a snowstorm one week, a wave of crime in its schools the next week, and a decision by the state or local government to shut down a city program in the third.

3
The Evolution of Problems and Policies

The fragmentation and street-fighting pluralism that characterize urban government exist in large part because of inherently fragmenting forces in the city. These characteristics have deep historical foundations. They have developed over time as a result of evolutionary changes in the urban political system. The present structure of urban government has been built by accretion. New additions have been added to the edifice layer by layer by earlier urban policy makers dealing with different demands and pressures and trying to correct different deficiencies in the structure they inherited.

City government has responded in the course of its development to three sorts of historical problems. The first problem is the fundamental one of building a viable structure of government in the city; historical efforts to make urban government work have tended, in fact, to increase the fragmentation of urban institutions.

The second historical problem, which reflects the city's distinctive service function, is that of ordering the relationship between those who deliver and receive services. Urban policy makers in this century have turned increasingly toward centralized, bureaucratic, professional control of service delivery as a way of establishing public control over what was perceived to be an inefficient and even anarchic system of service delivery. But this solution has not only failed to solve certain related problems in service delivery but has itself generated a new set of problems.

The third historical problem of urban policy making is that of trying to devise solutions to particular policy problems. City governments have had both remarkable successes and resounding failures in their problem solving. In addition, although city hall now deals routinely with many problems that once crippled the city (and that made the "good old days" look more like "bad old days"), urban policy makers today face a set of service problems that pose increasingly difficult social and political dilemmas. In looking at specific policy problems in historical perspective, we can see just how deeply reactive and erratic urban policy making has been over time.

Urban problems have both persisted and changed, and urban policy making has evolved while still retaining its fundamental characteristics. The problems of the present-day city are a subtle combination of old problems and new ones which have evolved in such a way as to make the city increasingly ungovernable.[1]

The Search for An Urban Political Order

Like most other historical political systems the urban policy began with a relatively simple governmental structure and with limited functions and pressures on it. In the colonial and pre–Civil War periods from 1760 to 1840, American cities were literally and figuratively "closed corporations."[2] They were literally so in the sense that only a small percentage of residents—property owners—were allowed to vote, and local governing bodies were typically controlled by a small, self-perpetuating group of city fathers. American cities were figuratively closed corporations in the sense that the early city fathers had little to do or even discuss beyond "minding the store" and preserving harmony in the body politic. More than anything urban politics in this period resembled the elite-dominated, status-quo-oriented village politics described by Arthur Vidich and Joseph Bensman in *Small Town in Mass Society*.[3] This was the Yankee era of social homogeneity, of crude public facilities, and of ragtag public services (such as the night watch and volunteer firemen). But even in this uncomplicated and undramatic period of governance, the roots of fragmentation were being sown. As the physical city grew, the centralized but passive caretaker government did little to establish public control over it. As a result both the city and its public institutions and services grew piecemeal. Newly developed areas received services and facilities as the need arose, and the consequence was geographical fragmentation of public control. Just outside the boundaries of the central-city areas, new cities and villages sprang up as urban settlements extended into farmland. This is the same pattern that we encounter today with the proliferation of suburban governments in metropolitan areas. The difference is that, by comparison to the present, this early urban political order was lilliputian, involving numerous tiny polities without the population to demand extensive services or the governmental machinery to provide them. This was a world of silent government, of city fathers running their cities and villages as closed corporations.

After 1840 this early political order was transformed by the massive immigration from Europe. The social impact of immigration is self-evident; relatively homogeneous communities became not only diverse but divided. The great machines of the nineteenth century were in large part the product of the ethnic division between Yankees and immigrants. As such they represented a waging of the social struggle by political means. The urban machine provided both material and symbolic benefits to the new immigrant population—patronage, an ombudsman-style linkage between city and citizen, and ethnic recognition. More important, at least in political terms, the urban machine emerged as one possible solution to the structural problems presented by the earlier political order. In the first place, the order presided over by the city fathers lacked political roots in the new urban community and thus provided little in the way of political and administrative communications between city and citizen. Indeed the political order, remote and out of touch with street-level needs in the early nineteenth century, clearly lacked the ability to adapt to the new service demands of an unfamiliar population. In this sense the machine was an experiment in political adaptation, an attempt to forge new political channels of communication between the city government and its citizens.[4] Equally important the machine sought to put an end to the progressive fragmentation of the urban political and administrative structure. As Robert Merton and others have noted one major effect of the great machines was to consolidate the scattered pieces of political power and to forge a new, coherent system of public control.[5] As it developed this system was increasingly characterized by corruption and graft; but where successful, it was also an enormously powerful instrument of centralized control. In its most dramatic incarnations—in Tammany Hall, Jersey City, and Kansas City, to name three machine cities—the new system led to political monopolies in the form of boss rule which established an entrenched structure of political control from city hall to the street corner.

The relationship between the machine order and the organization of service delivery is a little-explored subject but one that has crucial implications for the development of urban policy making. It is well known that the great machines provided personal services to immigrants needing assistance and mediation in dealing with a distant and unfamiliar government. This is the classic machine role vividly depicted by George Washington Plunkett, the shoestand philosopher of Tammany Hall, as well as by a modern counterpart, Edward Costikyan, the Tammany leader in the early 1960s.[6] Today, as the machines have declined, the need for a functional equivalent to the political linkage between citizens and ward leaders has led to the creation of neighborhood service centers, little city halls, and ombudsman experiments.

The machine also provided far more substantial benefits to a smaller group of residents: patronage jobs in a rapidly expanding public sector. Since the public sector grew as a result of the need to govern and deliver services to a dramatically expanded and diversified population, it can be said that the machine was at first the creation of immigration and then the creator of a new political order based on the impact of immigration on the structure of government. Immigration provided the political opportunity, and the machine provided the political innovation to capitalize on that opportunity. Immigration and the machine thus exist in a special historical relationship. The capacity of the machine to deliver the level of services and jobs necessary to establish extensive political control depended on the immigration-produced transformation of the social and governmental order. According to this analysis a political innovation like the machine could not be made in a period when the size of government was either fixed or contracting.

The success of the machine as a mechanism for public control depended also on the nature of the services that were demanded and supplied during its period of growth. The machine flourished by providing personal services and favors (which established political communication, trust, loyalty, and electoral support) and by undertaking large-scale public works, which generated large amounts of capital, produced highly visible benefits to the community, and led to the centralization of power and public control.

The new technology of traction, bridges, water supply, tunnels, subways, and the like required large bond issues, contracts, and expenditures. In turn, when controlled by the machine, these public works projects provided jobs in construction, administration, and maintenance, windfall profits for those who knew where the city was going to build, money in the city hall till (not all of which was spent on the projects), and the ability to reward political allies in the granting of government contracts. The task of building the physical structure of the city carried with it powerful political resources in the form of both capital and operating expenditures that could easily be translated into political money. The construction of large-scale public works also gave the machine a highly salient political product and thus the appearance of successfully delivering services to urban residents.

Perhaps most important the construction of large-scale public works required centralized coordination and administration—a function that the great machines were only too happy to provide. Whereas the simpler public services of an earlier period, such as street paving, were locality specific and could be provided on a fragmented, ad hoc basis, bridges, sewer systems, traction, and water and gas companies were economically and politically natural monopolies and could not easily be planned and administered under a fragmented system of public control. In this structural sense the impact of the machines and that of large-scale public works were complementary, for both had the purpose of tying the city together, articulating its many parts into a more coherent whole. But, as with its relationship to immigration, the machine grew strong by harnessing itself to those forces that were transforming the structure of the city, and it used those forces as its essential political resources in establishing public control.

Thus, the machine gained and centralized political power by providing both direct personal services and large-scale public goods. However, in important ways, this thrust toward political centralization did not eliminate the existing fragmentation of the service delivery structure. Although the machine sought to establish an intricate system of political links and obligations, it was little concerned with the administrative organization of public services. It was important to the machine's control that police commissioners as well as police captains be dues-paying members of the political organization, but the machine was not particularly concerned if the commissioners had little administrative control over their captains in the field. The slight evidence that exists on urban public institutions in the machine age suggests that district officials and field supervisors ran their subunits like small feudal barons and made their own special arrangements with local citizens and politicians as to how services would be delivered and as to which regulations would be enforced (or not enforced) against which group of citizens. This system of dispersed policy making and standard setting may indeed have allowed public employees to respond to local demands and mores, but it also continued and, in fact, deepened the fragmentation of service delivery created in the earlier era.

The reform reaction to the machine's political order is well known. The reformers' response to the machine's power and corruption was to break up the system of centralized power and establish strong administrative control over urban government. But there was a sharp conflict between these two purposes that had serious implications for the organization of service delivery. Reformers were interested in establishing two quite different kinds of public control—one negative and one positive. The negative form of public control was a desire to prevent monopolies of political power and, as in antitrust, to divide power deliberately by parceling it out to independent boards and comissions. The idea was to frustrate the machine's political larceny of the machine by locking power up in a series of separate governmental safe-deposit vaults. But once it achieved this kind of negative public control, it was structurally impossible for reformers to achieve the second, positive form of control: coherent administrative control over urban government and service delivery. Having divided power in the hope of taming it, there was no way simultaneously to achieve stronger and more coordinated public control of urban bureaucracies and service delivery. The political order of reform added new political fragmentation to the existing administrative fragmentation in the city.

The reform movement was clearly successful in some cities in disrupting the machine, but it had little impact on bureaucracies and thus on the organization of service delivery. The reform movement's only remedy for the daily problems of service delivery was the introduction of the merit system and, with it, the creation of a civil service. However, this policy reform was an instrument for controlling personnel recruitment and promotion, not an instrument for reorganizing the operating structure of city departments —creating new incentives and strategies in service delivery.

The coming of the New Deal also had a significant impact on the urban political structure. Much has been written about how New Deal social programs and services displaced the personal services provided by the machine and thus undermined the machine's political position. They also had another important and undeniable effect on urban government: the creation of new social programs at the national level led to a pluralization of the service delivery structure at the city level. This meant that a new layer was added to the existing loosely coordinated administrative structure. In terms of the administrative control of city government, the net effect of New Deal social innovation was to compound the problem of fragmentation, which had become a historical plague on urban management and service delivery. In addition the growth of federal involvement brought with it a further division of policy making in the design of urban services. While in the past the states were the cities' limited partners and overseers in organizing urban services, the emergence of the federal government created a more complex partnership and, indeed, a three-ring circus of shared and competing public control.[7]

In the urban political system that developed after 1940, many of the patterns that had existed earlier were repeated with slight variations, and there were also several unsuccessful attempts to reverse the existing pressures toward fragmented administration and service delivery. The city of the 1940s and early 1950s was a quieter and less-pressured place than it had been before and was to become later. Broadly this period was an unfamiliar interlude between European immigration and depression on the one hand and massive black migration on the other. In this comparatively static city the process of bureaucratization in urban institutions grew apace. The problem of service delivery at this time was how to consolidate and control the chaotic service bureaucracy. In this context the apparent solution was to increase administrative control in city hall headquarters and to strengthen the power of the mayor through strong mayor charters. The attempt was made to create sufficient centralized power to counteract the powerful centrifugal forces in the governmental system. The result was formal-legal efforts at centralization (charter revision) and the continued buildup of central office administration. Had the city remained relatively static, these measures might have proved effective. But these attempts at central bureaucratic control had the effect of building yet another layer of administration on top of the existing system and thus rendering the structure of city government even more complex and cumbersome. As David Rogers has shown, the centralization of the New York school system soon led to what many considered a bureaucratic labyrinth "downtown" at "110 Livingston Street."[8]

By the end of the 1950s it was becoming obvious to many mayors and citizens alike that urban problems were growing dramatically and that the city government lacked the capacity to deal with them. The city's housing stock, built during the period of immigration and rapid growth, was now old and decaying, and so were the main public facilities—schools, public transit, and even the water system. More important the migration of large numbers of poor blacks, Puerto Ricans, and Chicanos from rural areas placed new demands on existing social services and contributed to the rapid growth of central-city slums. Once again urban policy makers in America's large cities were reacting to new social and economic pressures in a highly unstable political environment.

Urban renewal was the federal government's initial response to this new awareness of an impending urban crisis.[9] Although the renewal program in no way solved the problem of spreading slums and blight, it did have a powerful impact on the structure of urban government in many cities, which can be seen most clearly in cities where renewal programs were most pronounced—New Haven, Atlanta, and Philadelphia. In these cities renewal led to an increased centralization of political power and to the rise of new bureaucratic machines serving as instruments of central control.[10] In the first place, renewal provided a new source of patronage and capital expenditures that translated into potent political resources in the hands of energetic mayors like Richard C. Lee of New Haven.[11] In addition, because it involved large-scale projects requiring coordination and control, renewal provided structural support for entrepreneurial, centralizing administrators just as earlier public works had for political bosses and parks and highway development did for Robert Moses in New York City, the now legendary "power broker" and "emperor of concrete."[12] It is entirely possible that Mayor Lee could have won election without renewal, but it was renewal that provided the dramatic, highly visible, and tangible issue that allowed him to dominate a city for almost two decades. And it was renewal that generated the staff expertise and patronage jobs required to build a bureaucratic machine in redevelopment agencies. In New Haven and other cities redevelopment agencies harnessed the centripetal pressures set in motion by renewal planning and became an increasingly dominant force in city administration.

The rise of urban regimes advancing ambitious renewal programs (and armed for this purpose with federal funds and new bureaucratic resources) had important consequences for the delivery of ordinary public services. This emphasis on bricks and mortar could not help but divert attention from social services, and the highly centralized, project-oriented renewal bureaucracies inhabited a political world far removed from the ordinary concerns of residents at the street level. In this period big projects drove out small ones, and large-scale thinking about the future of the city drove out small-scale thinking about the delivery of particular services to particular neighborhoods.

The political order based on urban renewal strengthened the power of mayors and established the power of redevelopment bureaucracies. But it did nothing to reduce the gap in political communication between city and citizen, and it did not reduce the fragmentation in the structure of service delivery. The new centralization and coordination of policy making in the redevelopment sector did not affect such other service delivery sectors, such as police and education.[13] However strong executive action might have been in the renewal arena, it was not aimed at the task of restructuring the organizational setting in which police captains, social workers, school principals, and sanitation foremen worked. In any case the structural barriers separating the different feudal baronies in service delivery were sufficiently strong to allow business to proceed as usual in schools and police stations.

The reaction to the rather imperial character of urban renewal was widespread. As J. Clarence Davies showed in the early 1960s, local residents began to protest against disruptive renewal plans, which they had no voice in determining.[14] They also began to demand that city government address itself to low-skilled, poorly educated, nonwhite immigrants in the center city. This demand was an evolutionary reaction to a political system preoccupied with bricks and mortar. Finally the demand for new and improved social services stemmed from the neighborhood view that public service bureaucracies were unresponsive, uncoordinated, and unaccountable. Thus, by this time, the problems of fragmentation and remoteness—the latter created by greatly expanded central offices —had finally come home to roost. And so, too, the lack of effective public control over service delivery had become a highly charged political issue.

If we understand the development of the urban political system as a reactive, evolutionary process in which adjustments designed to correct old problems also bring about new and unforeseen problems, we can easily see how the protest and community action movements of the 1960s were at once apparently logical solutions to the problem of unresponsiveness in service delivery and at the same time powerful contributors to the syndrome of ever-deepening fragmentation in urban government.

The community revolution rooted in the civil-rights movement and nourished by the war on poverty brought large numbers of new participants into the urban political arena and changed the relationship between city and citizen in many low-income urban neighborhoods.[15] At the least the various strategies of citizen participation in the late 1960s had the effect of creating a voluble neighborhood voice able to articulate complaints about public services and the unresponsiveness of service bureaucracies. This neighborhood voice, in turn, had the effect of establishing a dialogue between citizens and city agencies—a dialogue that had deteriorated progressively since the heyday of the machine and the ward heeler. The problem with this form of political communication was that it was adversary and largely one way. Community action was a strategy for fighting city hall, the schools, the housing authority, and the police. It was designed by its original architects in Washington, D.C., to provide creative conflict—to shake up remote and sluggish bureaucracies. The targets of protest in the existing government system were not without resources in dealing with protest groups from the community. Aside from straightforward delay and avoidance tactics, urban administrators under community pressure could always fall back on the fragmentation of the service delivery system by passing the buck to another agency or by relegating community demands to their own bureaucratic labyrinths.[16]

Interaction between citizens and city government typically evolved into a ritualized game of shadowboxing in which the political energies created by community action were largely consumed by the constant sparring with government. The shadowboxing game, as played in government, was a closed and hollow one. Instead of producing administrative efforts to deal with fundamental problems of service delivery, this game channeled administrative energy into the business of defending the government by dodging or parrying community demands and protests.

The community revolution also contributed to the fragmentation of administration and service delivery. With the development of protest groups and poverty programs, thousands of new neighborhood institutions were erected in American cities. Some community organizations disappeared as quickly as they grew up, and many of them were able to sink only very shallow political roots in their communities. The result was a diffusion of unrelated storefront organizations across urban neighborhoods. And since funding for community action typically provided for a few attractive staff positions in each organization, new but well-entrenched feudal barons were quickly added to the already crowded baronial structure in city politics.

Unlike urban renewal the community action program created strong centrifugal pressures on urban government. Whereas renewal sought to restructure the city viewed as a whole, community action was designed to improve urban life in particular neighborhoods. Because community action sought a multifaceted, locality-specific approach to service delivery, it also contributed to the growth of a diffuse antipoverty bureaucracy at the city hall level.[17]

The growth of poverty programs also brought with it a new federal and state involvement in urban policy making and thus further complicated and divided administrative power, authority, and responsibility for social service delivery. The federal government played a prominent role through the Office of Economic Opportunity in the development and evaluation of community antipoverty programs. Many states eventually entered the antipoverty arena, some creating departments of community affairs designed to focus and coordinate the services and programs provided through state government.

The decline, if not the final demise, of community action has stirred a heated debate about the cause of the program's failure. Whatever other factors may be pointed to, I would place primary emphasis on two kinds of fragmentation that have emerged out of the evolving urban administrative system. The first is that which exists both between different citizen groups at the street level and between citizens and city employees. The second—and equally important—kind of fragmentation is that which exists among federal, state, and city governments. The fragmentation at the street level and in the federal system is compounded by the weakness of the basic control mechanisms in urban bureaucracy.

During and immediately after the discordant experience of community action, many other experiments were tried out as cities continued to search for answers to their service delivery problems. On the one hand, community control was advanced as a dramatic and immediate solution to the perceived remoteness and unresponsiveness of city government. On the other hand, in New York City and elsewhere, the attempt was made to control service delivery by creating superagencies, that superimposed a new layer of even more centralized administration on top of the existing structure. Also in some cities the role of budget bureaus and analytical staff units was strengthened as another way of achieving central control. So, too, the model cities program rose and fell as an instrument of coordinated local planning, and more recently revenue sharing has been implemented—in large part as a way of consolidating administrative control in city hall.[18]

As with earlier urban solutions these experiments have not resolved the structural problems in the urban government that frustrate the development of an effective service delivery system.

Given the disappointing record of recent urban innovations, urban management remains very much in flux, and . . . control over service delivery still eludes the grasp of hard-pressed administrators.

With the benefit of considerable historical hindsight we can draw several conslusions about the evolution of the urban political order and its service delivery system. The evolutionary process has been marked by a sequence of governmental reactions to problems created in large measure by previous reactions. In this sense the development of urban management and service delivery has traced an erratic course between problem solving and problem creation. There are two important constants in this pattern of development. First, the urban political system has proved its adaptiveness in the face of massive social transformations. Both the machine and the community revolution were ingenious inventions of sidewalk politics designed to accommodate new pressures on the system. At the same time, despite its adaptiveness and ingenuity, urban administration has never come to terms with the steady growth of fragmentation in the city's service delivery system, and in fact the various new adaptations have often had the unforeseen consequence of deepening the syndrome of fragmentation.

The Control of Service Delivery

The second fundamental problem in the history of urban policy making has involved the search for both control and responsiveness in service delivery. The problem of control arose historically when fire protection was carried out by volunteer companies that viewed firefighting as a competitive sport and when each company had its own "gin steward" and received a five-dollar prize if it beat other companies to the fire.[19] This was also a time when teachers were often political patronage appointments; when garbage collection was carried out erratically by "scavengers";[20] when nurses were untrained (and some were prostitutes and drug addicts); when social workers were volunteers operating according to informal principles and practices.

How could city government control such a ragtag corps of street-level bureaucrats? The police in particular present a vivid example of the tenuous control that city administrators held over their foot soldiers. When city police were first established, policemen on the beat communicated with superior officers only in "face-to-face meetings or by messengers."[21] In later years, according to Jonathan Rubenstein:

Once the men were dismissed from roll call, their supervisors had no certain way of controlling what they did during their tour of work. The sergeants, who were called roundsmen in Philadelphia, frequently assigned men "meets"; prearranged times and places where the supervisors could visually check on them. The only way a roundsman had of discovering what his men were doing was to follow them around and make inquiries among the people who lived and worked on the beats. If he wanted to watch a man at work, he could, and frequently did, accompany him, but this obliged him to neglect other duties. The men were also isolated from each other, and their only way of attracting attention in moments of distress was by swinging the large rattles which city policemen had been carrying since the sixteenth century.[22]

Even with the steady improvement of communications technology, the problem of police supervision persisted and indeed made widespread corruption possible. Call boxes followed telegraph networks, and radio cars followed both. Various "pulling" systems have been adopted, and horns, colored lights, and bells have been employed to "attract a patrolman to his box for special messages."[23] But no amount of communications can place the policemen under direct, constant control. Policemen have continued to sleep on the job, take bribes, react to dangerous situations, beat up suspects, and occasionally be assaulted, and there is still precious little that police officials can do to regulate these varied encounters.

It is not only because of their inherent freedom and discretion that the mayor's foot soldiers are so hard to supervise and control. Equally important the foot soldiers have long treated the relationship between the servers and the served as a form of free market exchange. Writing of nineteenth-century New York City, Seymour Mandelbaum provides a telling account of the urban service provider as entrepreneur: "Many government officers acted as political entrepreneurs, selling their services directly to the public. Entrepreneurship over and beyond the law gave New York an unenviable reputation for corruption. Entrepreneurship was, however, written in the law itself as the complement of the conception of public action for limited private benefits. Those who received services should pay for them. Coroner, the county sheriff, the minor judiciary recorder, and court clerks were all recompensed by direct fees. The Chamberlain assumed responsibility for the safety of public funds, and in return, was allowed to keep the interest on city bank deposits in his pocket."[24]

In a classical bureaucracy employees are supposed to follow and apply simple rules and procedures about which there is little misunderstanding or disagreement. But in the world the city's street-level bureaucrats inhabit, there is usually little clarity or agreement about the nature of the service problem or its appropriate solution. What is an intolerable vice to one segment of the community may be a pleasurable pastime or a source of employment for others. And so the policeman has to deal with numbers runners, prostitutes, owners of after-hours bars, and the like with the knowledge that citizen demands and preferences are sharply divided and that the practitioners of "vice" are willing to pay a great deal for a covert police license to do business. What is a clean street for one urban resident is a civic disgrace to another.

Which standards are followed by garbagemen and what criteria does he use in picking up ashcans, street litter, improperly packaged garbage, bulk refuse, and trash from vacant lots? The problem is an old one, as the following administrative guideline from an early treatise on urban service delivery suggests: "Small dead animals are considered to be refuse, large dead animals are treated differently."[25]

Given the complexity and ambiguity of these service problems, the lack of clear-cut rules dealing with them, and the absence of a controlling hierarchy that would tightly constrain his descretion, the urban foot soldier handled many service demands through mutual bargaining and adjustment.[26] Instead of arresting the drunk or rowdy adolescents, the policeman told them to move on. Instead of closing down a dirty restaurant or a deteriorating house, the health or housing inspector issued only minor complaints on the promise that improvements would be made. Add the element of cynicism and greed on the part of public officials and the willingness of citizens to buy indulgences, and one can easily see how a full-scale exchange system developed in American cities. Mandelbaum again makes the central point: "Decentralized decision-making was embedded in both the values and the practice of the city. The most common form of decentralization—and simplification—was reliance upon the free practices of the market. Tweed's purchases of political support and his thievery were simply the ultimate extension of the dominance of the dollar-vote."[27]

Thus in the history of American cities, services have often not been delivered so much as they have been bought, sold, and negotiated. In a very real way this system of mutual adjustment and bargaining over services was an effective method of coordinating the supply and demand for services and an ingenious adaptation to the conflicting demands and chaotic circumstances of urban service delivery. But given the obvious imperfections of this rough-and-ready service market (for example, policemen could easily establish extortion cartels, and drug pushers, youth gangs, and prostitutes could easily inflict serious harm on third parties), bargaining and exchange between citizens and public servants were and are inadequate devices for ordering the delivery of urban services. Abuse was easy, and the system thus led to the development of systematic police corruption, aided the growth of organized crime, and demoralized citizens who either could not pay for services and indulgences or who were the victims of protected, illegal enterprise.

Service delivery has also been hard to control because urban service bureaucracies have had complex, confused, and overlapping missions. In some cities the police administered welfare programs and dispensed free soup, and in Boston during the 1820s they were responsible for the maintenance of streets and sewers.[28] According to one nineteenth-century report in New York the police were supposed to

preserve the public peace, prevent crime, detect and arrest offenders, suppress riots, mobs, and insurrections, disperse unlawful or dangerous assemblages, and assemblages which obstruct the free passage of public streets, sidewalks, parks, and public places; protect the rights of persons and property, guard the public health, preserve order at elections and all public meetings and assemblages; regulate the movement of teams and vehicles in streets, bridges, squares, parks, and public places, and remove all nuisances in the public streets, parks and public places; arrest all street mendicants and beggars; provide proper police attendance at fires; assist, advise, and protect emigrants, strangers, and travellers in public streets, at steamboat and ship landings and at railroad stations; carefully observe and inspect all places of public amusement, all places of business having excise or other licenses to carry on any business; all houses of ill-fame or prostitution, and houses where common prostitutes resort or reside; all lottery offices, policy shops, and places where lottery tickets or lottery policies are sold and offered for sale; all gambling houses, cock pits, rat pits, and public common dance houses, and to repress and restrain all unlawful or disorderly conduct or practices therein; enforce and prevent the violation of all laws and ordinances in force in said city; and for these purposes to arrest all persons guilty of violating any law or ordinance for the suppression or punishment of crime or offenses.[29]

The response of urban policy makers to this control problem was to centralize and professionalize service bureaucracies. In particular a strong professional ethos arose in service delivery, an ethos that emphasized scientific management, training, specialization, and meritocratic criteria of recruitment and promotion. The rise of professionalism among teachers, social workers, and policemen can be understood in part as a strategy for increasing the status of these occupations. Even more important the ethos of professionalism contained a strong political judgment that service delivery should not be based on an exchange of mutual adjustment with citizens but on the authority and expertise of those who deliver services. Marvin Lazerson has written thus of the Boston school system:

The commitment to public education was paralleled by the growth of professionalization and bureaucracy. . . . The Massachusetts teachers association, organized in 1847, gave educators greater influence as an interest group and higher status as professionals. Teacher certification laws were passed in the 1850's, establishing for the first time clear standards of entry and providing a basis for a permanent class of teachers. Closely related to these developments was the emergence of bureaucratic structures designed to bring order to increasingly complex urban school systems. Record gathering—attendance, expenditures, teacher-pupil ratios—assumed major importance, the dissemination of statistics providing for comparative analysis of school systems. Supervision and administration were centralized and made prominent in the daily workings of the schools.[30]

This ethos would have perhaps been enough in itself to drive urban administration toward greater centralization. But in the search for the substance of professionalism, the ethos became linked up with the principles of scientific management, differentiation, and efficiency that held sway in business administration.

For the police chief or school superintendent trying to gain some rough mastery over his diffuse and often chaotic service system, the apparent ability of business techniques to create efficient management carried a powerful message. And so public managers, preaching professionalism, reached for methods that worked in industry and sought to produce a strongly hierarchical system through the progressive centralization of power and control. As Michael Katz put it: "Schoolmen over and over again used the example of industry as an idealized standard that formed the basis for their justifications of the superintendency. They often described their school systems as factories and used metaphors based on the composition and the mechanism. Modern industry, they could see, had developed its remarkable capacity through a rational organization that stressed hierarchy, the division of labor, and intensive professional supervision. If those methods worked in industries as diverse as textiles and railroads, why would they not work in education."[31]

The drive toward central bureaucracy and professionalism was pressed vigorously. A variety of new "bureaucratic innovations were introduced as part of a continuing process of rationalizing and coordinating the increasingly complex school system."[32] One such change concerned job security for teachers: "To perfect their hierarchies, schoolmen argued it was necessary to carry the development of career lines with school systems even further . . . when all teachers were offered a career, security, and protection from arbitrary dismissal, schoolmen asserted, hierarchical systems, would be nearly perfect."[33] But the result was not the smoothly efficient system that was envisioned—at least in the Boston school system: "When bureaucracy arises in piecemeal fashion, as it did in Boston, the demarcation of duties and lines of authority becomes blurred, and tensions arising from overlapping functions are almost inevitable. In Boston, this problem was exacerbated by the sloppy way in which the school board went about the process of organization-building."[34] The realization came much later that it was possible to centralize the form of service delivery—through the development of large-scale central bureaucracies—without centralizing actual control over the intricate exchange relationship at the street level.

Three other aspects of the professional ethos had important effects in shaping the structure of urban service delivery. First, at the core of professionalism lies the notion of standards. While amateur administrators may be content to make ad hoc, pragmatic policies, the professional wished to establish explicit and uniform rules of conduct that made clear how a trained policeman, teacher, or fireman should behave in delivering services. To set uniform standards in this way was to upgrade and to rise above ad hoc, haphazard judgments. It was also, as it turned out, to impose inflexible rules, to eliminate discretion from the deeply discretionary work of urban foot soldiers. The result of standard setting was thus to codify, to proliferate regulations-reporting procedures. Nevertheless the drive to set standards did not and could not guarantee that standards were met in substance as well as in form.

The professional ethos also entailed the belief that professionals possessed some special sort of trained discipline or expertise that would permit them to do their job better than amateurs. The fact that such expertise might be mythical did not deter the emerging service professionals. They latched on to what they could find in the way of "scientific" theory and proclaimed their expertise on the basis of adherence to scientific methods. Nowhere was this dynamic more vivid than in the rise of the social work profession. When it operated as a volunteer service, with untrained personnel working in settlement houses and making home visits, social work had a strong missionary flavor and stressed empathy, personal contact, informal helping techniques, and, of course, moral uplift. The new social work professionals reacted against the "lady bountiful" image of volunteer do-gooders, against what they saw as intuitive, sentimental altruism, and against the haphazard procedures of private charity organizations. The social work professionals found in psychoanalytical theory and systematic bureaucratic organization precisely the scientific theory and method of operation that they were looking for. As Roy Lubove has written:

A major source of irritation to social workers anxious to elevate their professional status consisted of those "many popular misunderstandings of social work, which identify it with nursing, with mental testing, with occupational therapy, with neighborliness." Psychiatry in the early twentieth century played a significant role in strengthening the social worker's conviction that she offered a distinct and valuable service which required specialized skill and training. Important links were forged between psychiatry and social work before the Freudian penetration of the 1920's. Toward the end of the nineteenth century a new kind of psychiatry, receptive to social service, launched a new casework speciality and a quest for professional function and skill in new institutional settings.[35]

In practice a major result of this professional approach was to emphasize the meticulous reporting and regulation of services. More important, the emphasis on treatment tended to replace the personalized "good neighbor" relationship of paternalistic charity with a more impersonal and aloof professional-patient relationship. The emphasis on the scientific organization of charity markedly increased the formal, bureaucratic content of the relationship between the servers and the served. The test of service delivery was professional "method": "The quest for efficiency and administrative technique in social agency operations paralleled the caseworker's efforts to reduce the range of intuition, subjectivity, and unpredictability in her own work. In both cases the volunteer introduced an element of uncertainty. Neither her livelihood nor social status depended upon conformity to agency policy or to the standards and procedures of professional casework. Volunteer service conflicted with the administrator's desire for rational, efficient organization and the social worker's identification with the agency as a vehicle for professional achievement."[36]

Along with the emphasis on expertise and bureaucratic organization, professionalism also carried with it a strong impetus toward specialization of tasks and responsibilities in service delivery. Specialization meant the rise in police departments of a large detective bureau and, within the bureau, of vice detectives, narcotics detectives, and the like. In education it meant the rise of department chairmen, assistant principals, assistant superintendents for curriculum development, and so forth. This division of labor might simply be a curiosity of administrative organization if it did not substantially affect the role and status of the foot soldiers at the street levels—the patrolmen, teachers, and firemen. With increased specialization the patrolman and classroom teacher were no longer the central figures in service delivery; rather they were lower-level bureaucrats in a hierarchical system that rewarded the more specialized detectives and school administrators and thus created strong incentives for the most able to leave street-level work for the detective bureau or the central board of education. For these reasons specialization implied a different sort of centralization— one that drew talent away from the street level by conferring benefits and status not on the skillful daily work with citizens but on the basis of technical, administrative, and investigative expertise. With this set of organizational incentives it is little wonder that the foot soldiers who walk the beat or teach first grade are viewed (and view themselves) not as valued generalists but as the "dirty workers" of urban government. It is only recently that police chiefs and school superintendents have recognized this paradox in service delivery —that the most crucial employees are the least rewarded—and have sought to upgrade the role of patrolmen (vis-à-vis detectives) and to reward effective teaching (for example, through the creation of master teachers).

The drive to control service delivery through centralized administration was also aided by the development of new technologies. At first the technologies involved in service delivery reinforced the fragmented pattern of service delivery. When policemen lacked devices for communicating with central headquarters, when the streets were cleaned by wandering public scavengers, and when fire companies had limited mobility and limited communication, it was intrinsically difficult to establish a centralized control of municipal operations. As service technology developed, so did the capacity for and, in some cases, the actual extent of centralized bureaucratic control. Basic technological improvements like the telephone obviously increased the possibility of central surveillance. The introduction of public reservoirs, almshouses, and hospitals all served to consolidate previously atomized services. The development of record-keeping technologies, culminating in the computer, gave substance to the idea of a bureaucratic system. In addition the decline of voluntary service organizations and the rise of federal welfare programs also strongly reinforced the trend toward centralization.

The development of urban services had been characterized by a steady movement from private voluntary action to public control. As the demand for services increased in cities, private organizations and charities that pioneered social and educational services were replaced by government agencies. This meant an increased centralization of service delivery when, for example, a settlement house based in and oriented to a particular neighborhood was replaced by a city-wide welfare department.

The growth of federal social programs, beginning before 1932 but powered by the large-scale interventions of the New Deal, further centralized the design and fiscal control of service delivery. Service arrangements that were once negotiated by street-level employees and citizens were now to a significant extent redefined by directives from the federal government and were expanded, reorganized, or superseded by new service delivery mechanisms as a result of a more distant bargaining process between federal, state, and local officials.

In the face of professionalism, the centralizing effect of new technologies, and federal intervention, the street-level world of service delivery was largely transformed. But more important than the growth of central administration was the failure of that new structure to achieve administrative control over the day-to-day operation of urban foot soldiers. Whatever might be said about educational policy or criminal justice in Washington, D.C., or about professionalism and efficiency in city hall, service delivery still depended ultimately on the individual policeman, teacher, fireman, garbageman, and social worker who represent and indeed embody the abstract ideas of government and social policy at the street level. The creation of large-scale bureaucratic systems also left unsolved the fundamental problem in service delivery of how to control the behavior of the mayor's foot soldiers. Even with administrative centralization, it was no less difficult to prevent corruption, bargaining exchange, erratic performance, and the other perceived failings that stimulated reform in the first place. What bureaucratic centralization could and did do was to make the service delivery system more cumbersome, rigid, and remote. Centralization could insure that service delivery was not intentionally hand-tailored to varied neighborhood interests and/or explicitly based on ad hoc exchanges and accommodations; but it could not prevent the old arrangements from continually slipping in through the back door. The persistence of police corruption, erratic garbage collection, and highly differentiated teaching methods and welfare regulation is strong evidence on this point. In addition it is important to understand the costs to service delivery of professionalism, bureaucratization, and federal intervention. Professionalism tended to increase the distance between foot soldiers and citizens, making policemen and teachers less part of the community they served and more members of a separate professional guild. Bureaucratization increased the complexity and formality of procedures and communication channels between city government and its citizens. Federal intervention had the effect also of increasing the complexity of administration and, in particular, of diverting administrative energy in city hall away from what was going on below and focusing it on what was going on above.

The problem of responsiveness in service delivery has traced a quite different pattern of historical development. The weakly controlled exchange systems of nineteenth-century service delivery may well have contributed to responsiveness and mutual trust in the service relationship. This was a different, more positive feature of urban fragmentation, which had the effect of making urban neighborhoods the only cohesive political and social unit in the city. Service delivery was organized around neighborhood police precincts and firehouses. The political organization of the great machines also was based on the small neighborhood unit assigned to the wardheeler. Ethnic and racial groups established their own enclaves around neighborhood churches and social clubs.

Fifty years ago policemen walked the beat, and teachers and other urban employees were likely to live near the places where they worked. Although it is hard to demonstrate (except in the case of policemen), urban foot soldiers at the turn of the century were almost certainly visible, better known, and more rooted in the communities they served than all their successors today. The same forces that created strong neighborhood ties in the nineteenth-century immigrant city also enhanced the ties between urban residents and public employees. Of those forces toward cohesion—

and they are undoubtedly various—two must be considered central.

In the first place, in the nineteenth-century city dominated by new immigrants, the living conditions of citizens and public employees tended to be roughly similar. Teachers, policemen, and garbagemen were likely to understand from their own experience what was going on in the neighborhoods where they worked. The streets, housing, and people of the neighborhood were in this sense recognizable and familiar. What is more important, the urban foot soldiers often had ethnic ties with the people they served. This is manifestly true of the Irish policeman working in a predominantly Irish neighborhood, and if the demand for new urban employees was filled generally by recent immigrants, it must have been true for many other foot soldiers as well.

What emerges from this account of the immigrant city of the nineteenth century is a kind of social symmetry in service delivery. More precisely the relationship between servers and the served was roughly symmetrical when the former shared the same neighborhood, living conditions, and ethnic ties with the latter. What is important about this is that it would be obviously supportive of the personal, even intimate, role that exists between citizens and urban service delivers. Indeed it can be argued that the destruction of this symmetry caused a commensurate deterioration in service delivery because policemen, social workers, and teachers, unlike state department officials or state highway administrators, necessarily are involved in personal and family problems and generally operate well within their clients' private domain. It follows that trust is a central ingredient in good service delivery. If urban foot soldiers are to operate effectively in a close personal relationship with clients, they cannot be mistrusted. And they are likely to be strongly mistrusted if they are seen as alien, prejudiced, or ignorant of their clients' living conditions. Viewed in this way, there is a strong relationship between social symmetry, trust, and effective service delivery. If so, a decline in social symmetry would adversely affect trust and, in turn, service delivery.

It is very clear that social symmetry has been notably absent in service delivery in the large American city since 1960. Policemen, teachers, firemen, and other public employees tend to be white and working class and not residents of the port-of-entry neighborhoods where the nonwhite immigrants arrived. The social bond between the servers and the served has thus to a large extent been destroyed, and from this analysis it is no surprise that feelings of mistrust, hostility, and alienation have grown rapidly among nonwhite urban residents. Thus not only is city government overly centralized, cumbersome, and remote, but its services are delivered by people who are often incapable of successfully entering into direct, personal service relationships with their new clients. On the other hand, the mayor's foot soldiers also suddenly were forced to work in an unfamiliar, hostile, and threatening urban world. Policemen and teachers who knew their way around the old white neighborhoods because they had grown up in them (or ones like them) were now faced with angry demands and protests and with the loss of community support and approval. They are often viewed as victims by their families and by sympathetic observers, and as "pigs" by unsympathetic clients. Not only did the social symmetry between the servers and the served dissolve in the 1960s, but so did the social norms that public employees and other citizens had come to expect in urban life. The sudden rise in muggings, drug addiction, gang warfare, assaults on policemen, and other forms of antisocial behavior shocked many white residents and helped to provoke the urban crisis mentality. Because of this highly visible decline in what might be called normal social conduct, urban problems that were not nearly as pervasive or intense as in the nineteenth century caused a far worse crisis. White public employees and their neighbors in the white communities may or may not have been deeply racist; but they clearly were angry and fearful about social changes (especially black migration) that were linked with crime, violence, and the disruption of familiar community patterns.

This decline in social agreement about basic norms and behavior was also expressed in more subtle forms. The accounts in urban histories and administrative textbooks about the policeman, teacher, or social worker who could tell a "good kid" from a bad one and act accordingly presumed an intimate understanding on the part of the foot soldier not only of particular individual residents but also of the appearances, life-styles, and attitudes of urban residents. When residents become unfamiliar, even alien, to the deliverers of services, the capacity of policemen and teachers to make careful distinctions on the basis of subtle cues is vastly reduced. In the extreme case all sixteen-year-old black males wearing apple hats came to look like probable assailants to policemen unfamiliar with a neighborhood and the people in it. With increased social distance residents are less able to interpret the behavior and attitudes of public employees. What the foot soldiers may think of as tough but fair conduct may appear to be blatant racism to nonwhite residents. Indeed it has often been reported that many charges of police brutality do not involve physical force at all but rather the perception on the part of residents that police behaved in an insulting way, made implicit racial slurs, or failed to treat nonwhites with due respect. On the other hand policemen, teachers, and other foot soldiers easily take strongly expressed demands, grievances, and protests about services to be hostile acts, direct personal attacks on them and their institutions.

The result of this progressive estrangement between the servers and the served has been mutually destructive stalemate. The served could not make their voices heard or have their services improved. The servers cannot gain respect or regain a sense of mastery and security. In the absence of this fundamental social communication, residents throw bottles at firemen, and policemen "beat heads."

Urban Problem Solving

Edward Banfield presents a serious challenge to present-day prophets of urban doom. In the course of arguing that there is no urban crisis, he suggests that in many ways the city has never had it so good. At one point he comments that "in many important respects the material conditions of life in the cities have long been improving."[37] His point is valid to the extent that we forget how poor conditions and services were in the nineteenth-century city. In 1880 the *Chicago Times* made the following appraisal of urban life in Chicago: "The river stinks. The air stinks. People's clothing permeated by the foul atmosphere stinks. . . . No other word expressed it so well as stink. A stench means something finite. Stink reaches the infinite and becomes sublime in the magnitude of odiousness."[38] Nor was this appraisal at all unusual. According to another account a pedestrian in early nineteenth-century St. Louis "could not walk more than a few paces without having his 'nerves assailed by the putrid carcasses of Hogs, Dogs, etc.' that cluttered the pathways."[39] According to a more grisly account, the sidewalk held the following horrors: "the heads of sheep, lambs, etc., the heap of cattle, blood, and offal strewed in the gutters and sometimes on the pavement dead dogs, cats, rats, and hogs."[40]

Refuse and putrid carcasses were not the only, or even the most visible, problems. According to one street-level account, in large cities vagrant children roamed the streets and "picked rags, sold goods, blacked boots, begged money, picked pockets, stole, and some girls turned to prostitution."[41] Groups of young ruffians also roamed through the neighborhoods and often ruled the streets. In Lewis Yablonsky's phrase the gangs "were apparently in charge of their own territory."[42] Certainly the police were not in charge— either of the gangs or the streets. In his portrait *Gangs of New York* Herbert Ashbury describes how police, if they were foolish enough to intervene in gang fighting, were quickly "subdued": "A lone policeman, with more courage than judgment, tried to club his way through the mass of struggling men and arrest the ring leaders, but he was knocked down, his clothing stripped from his body, and he was fearfully beaten with his own nightstick. He crawled through a plunging mob to the sidewalk, and, naked except for a pair of cotton drawers, ran to the Metropolitan headquarters in White Street, where he gasped out the alarm and collapsed. A squad of policemen was dispatched to stop the rioting, but when they marched bravely up Center Street the gangs made common cause against them, and they were compelled to retreat after a bloody encounter in which several men were injured."[43]

In other ways, too, the nineteenth-century city was unrecognizably primitive and perilous by present standards. There was a distinct peril that ox carts would lose control and kill children on the sidewalks. Fire and communicable diseases were a clear and present danger to all residents of large cities. As Sam Bass Warner, Jr., put it, "Sheer numbers, onrushing growth, and the crowding of land broke down the earlier small-town checks against fire and communicable disease. In every American city devastating fires swept whole blocks of valuable downtown districts. The Chicago Fire of 1871 was but the most celebrated of a half century of conflagration. Contaminated walls, overused and ill-tended privies, overcrowded buildings and rooms, and shiploads of undernourished and sick immigrants brought epidemic waves of cholera, typhus, and yellow fever which swept the downtown districts of the poor, seeped into hotels and public places, and frightened all classes of city dwellers."[44]

The threat of street crime, then called highway robbery, was a constant companion of the urban pedestrian. Cities used severe measures to combat this urban "state of nature." Carl Bridenbaugh points out that in 1761 highway robbery was punished by death.[45] Official corruption was rampant; it permeated red-light districts, traction, and public works, and even public schools were characterized by patronage appointments and various forms of graft. Control of the schools was franchised to local machine politicians.[46]

These unheavenly urban problems were found in cities of all sizes and regions, and their incidence can be traced back to the beginning of the eighteenth century. Richard Wade found:

By 1815 Western towns had witnessed the appearance of all the urban problems which confronted Eastern cities, and already these questions exerted a growing pressure on local governments. In nearly every field of municipal authority—police, fire, streets, water, and health—conditions deteriorated so rapidly that a series of emergencies appeared, requiring decisive action. Any one of these was grave enough to tax the ingenuity of local authorities, yet the crises came on many fronts. Indeed, the multiplicity of issues was the real danger. Communities could handle some of the challenges, but not all. Yet their interrelatedness made success in any single one difficult.[47]

Early Urban Services

Any analysis of the evolution of service delivery must necessarily begin with the early nineteenth century at the time when urban services, as we know them today, were first being systematically developed in American cities. Organized, large-scale public services have been a feature of the urban landscape for little more than a hundred years. (The precise point of origin differs, of course, with the service and the city.) In the eighteenth and early nineteenth centuries the typical American city had only the most primitive public facilities and services. The streets—many of which were unpaved—were the domain of pigs and dogs (alive and dead) as well as pedestrians and horses, no mean source of pollution themselves. The job of garbage collection was left to unreliable contractors, scavengers, and the pigs. With few exceptions there was no public water supply, and sellers of "tea water" from the few freshwater wells did a brisk business peddling their precious commodity from door to door. Firefighting was the province of volunteer companies who often competed with one another more than they fought fires, and, in any case, they were effective only when they could find sufficient water. (With the development of crude water mains, firefighting improved as firemen were able to tap into the main through wooden fireplugs.) In short, the city's firefighters did not inspire confidence.

A wave of excitement and agitation followed each big blaze, and constructive steps often resulted. But each new outbreak found the town somewhat unprepared. The engines worked badly or not at all, volunteers arrived too late, or bystanders preferred to watch the flames rather than fight them. Efforts to improve equipment and techniques could not be sustained after public interest lagged and money ran low. An old hand at fire reform finally became convinced that people enjoyed the spectacle and did not want improvement. Retreating into satire, he proposed two schemes to indulge their appetites. The first, called "plan dilatory," required the government to burn all its apparatus so that no one need fear that the show might be stopped. His alternative, "plan Immediate," stipulated that the city should buy twelve houses annually from a "conflagration fund," and light one every month as a kind of civic celebration.[48]

In the early nineteenth century police protection was equally haphazard, having only recently emerged from the era of the night watch and the rattle. In 1865 only the seven largest cities had police forces.[49] According to one study: "Lexington [Kentucky] authorities, for instance, received constant complaints about the 'improprieties,' 'delinquency,' and 'sundry misdemeanors and neglect of duty' of their men. Teenagers and rowdies loved to 'bait the watch,' and even adults obstructed their work. In no town in 1815 were the police strong enough to quell riots or major disorders, or even stop waves of vandalism."[50]

Public schooling was a halting experiment in New York City's free schools and merely an idea in most other cities. Organized health and hospital care took place mainly in almshouses. Conditions in the first hospitals were clearly rudimentary: "In many institutions the poor were crowded two and three in a bed and nursing care was minimal. Bedclothes were seldom changed and the attendants were often of the lowest class. Prostitutes and petty criminals who could no longer practice their trades could often eke out a living in hospitals. Hospital nurses, other than members of religious orders, were considered the dregs of society; and it was for this reason that Florence Nightingale and her disciples insisted on rigid, puritanical codes in establishing the early nursing schools. If nursing was to appeal to a higher class of women, it must first be made respectable."[51] The almshouses themselves were beginning to replace home care and the alleys and cellars where the poor and mentally ill were sequestered. Public transportation was limited to the omnibus—a kind of horsedrawn jitney—and later to the horse-drawn streetcar, and the "living" conditions on both were widely felt to be appalling. There were almost no parks and recreation areas in the city. As one opponent of municipal parks put it, "God taught children to play."[52]

Various attempts by the city government to deal with problems through the development of regulations proved ineffective and underscored the weakness of city government. One study found that "a decade after publication of the report in 1857 on conditions in New York, a Tenement House Law attempted to impose limits on the number of people a building could accommodate, and in 1887 further regulation required inside plumbing and fire escapes. Both laws proved unenforceable; in 1890 some 30,000 tenement buildings in Manhattan contained over a million people. The building codes adopted in other big cities were equally ineffective."[53] More generally Richard Wade has shown that "poor enforcement was a familiar lament in every city."[54] He recorded the view of the *Kentucky Reporter* in 1809: "We have had Hog Laws, Dog Laws, Theatre Laws, and Laws about Hay Scales . . . Kitchen Slops, Soap

Suds, and Filth of every kind, and in no single instance have they been executed."[55]

Urban Progress

To place the current failures of urban problem solving into historical perspective and to appraise the extent to which the city is now or ever has been ungovernable, it is useful to construct a balance sheet of the past successes and failures of urban problem solving to see what kinds of problems cities have been able to deal with successfully; which have been apparently solved only to reappear in a new form, with the past solution becoming an essential part of the new problem; and which have proved completely intractable.

With some notable exceptions the problems of urban policy making are not new, and for that reason we cannot evaluate governmental programs and policies in a historical vacuum. Are modern mayors doing a particularly poor job of governing their cities and solving their policy problems? Are the city's problems increasingly difficult and complex? These questions clearly compel historical comparisons. The idea of the ungovernable city has substance only if we can show large, persistent deficits over time in the balance sheet of urban problem solving. In addition the idea that the modern city is ungovernable gains force if we can show further that the urban problems that persist and those that have arisen in recent decades are especially intractable.

First let us look to the historical record of successful urban problem solving. Considering the magnitude and variety of nineteenth-century urban problems, the performance of city government in many areas of policy and service delivery was impressive, if not remarkable. As Moses Rischin put it, "Only prodigious feats in engineering and construction enabled the city to service New Yorkers. . . . Street improvements, water and gas pipes, telegraph and telephone lines, and all means of transport were crammed upon less than one dozen thoroughfares."[56] To construct the physical infrastructure of a rapidly expanding city, urban governments were forced to increase their expenditures massively. Writing in 1904, Frank Goodnow noted that "a good method of judging [the] degree of this extension of the sphere of municipal activity is to be found in the expenditures of cities. The total expenditure of New York at the present time (1904) is something more than $150,000,000 annually and this sum was in 1898 equaled by the aggregate expenditures of the seven other cities of 400,000 population in the country."[57]

In 1902 Charles Zueblin published *American Municipal Progress,* which set out in detail the accomplishments of cities—large and small—throughout the country. The subheadings of his chapters give a strong flavor of the nature of this early "urban progress." They include smoke abatement, street cleaning, waste disposal, mosquito control, snow removal, municipal hospitals for infectious diseases, five-platoon police systems, juvenile courts, school nurses, vacation schools, public libraries, public baths, playgrounds, city surveys, libraries, municipal utilities, parks, social centers, school lunches, municipal employment bureaus, kindergartens, high-pressure fire service systems, public transit, street lighting, sewage systems, traffic police, municipal markets, public drinking fountains, water supply, correctional institutions, and municipal lodging houses.

These categories suggest four kinds of development in urban problem solving: (1) the development of new technologies as in street lighting, street cleaning, and high-pressure fire systems; (2) the development of new or expanded public works as in public transit, parks, playgrounds, and reservoirs; (3) the development of new public institutions and methods of organization as in public utilities, libraries, and juvenile courts, as well as the paramilitary organization of street cleaners and public patrols; and (4) the development of innovative public programs such as school lunches, kindergartens, and social centers. In general these signs of progress reflect an era when physical construction and the building of new public institutions were the preeminent activities of urban government. The energy and ingenuity embodied in these urban initiatives should not be understated. Consider the following examples.

The improvement and protection of the water supply enabled cities to bring typhoid under control. "It is estimated in Pittsburgh that the filtration of the water of the Allegheny River is annually saving 7000 typhoid cases (sordidly estimated at $150 per case) and

500 lives (measured at $5000 per life)—a total of three and one-half million. The reason for making this commercial statement of life values is that such economy for two years covers the cost of installing the filter plant. The filtration of water in Philadelphia reduced the typhoid rate in less than a decade to one-fifth or one-sixth its former proportions."[58]

Through municipal ownership cities were able to construct public transportation systems: "The municipal ownership of the Boston subway has been profitable to the city, not burdensome to the operating company, and represents the least a city can do that protects its streets for the people.

"The total investment to June 30, 1913, in publicly constructed and owned subways in Boston, is twenty-two million dollars. The subways (with the exception of the Cambridge tunnel) are all in an area not over two miles square. They focus transportation coming from all directions and reaching the subways by a dozen entrances.

"Boston now owns a twenty-six million dollar subway system by which it controls an eighty-two million dollar transportation system."[59]

Although few cities had playgrounds of any kind at the end of the nineteenth century, they sprang up rapidly and in large numbers after 1900. "The Playground and Recreation Association of America in 1913 reported 342 cities with 2400 playgrounds in charge of 6000 paid supervisors. Nearly $6,000,000 was spent in administering these playgrounds in that year, and twenty cities were planning to spend over $2,000,000 on equipment in 1914. The playgrounds are becoming training schools for their attendants after the manner of the libraries. Large numbers of these communities conduct only summer playgrounds, but 152 cities reported over 600 centers open in the evening. Seventy-one cities kept their playgrounds open all the year, employing nearly 600 workers."[60]

In some service areas city governments indeed were able to end the early anarchy, developing well-organized bureaucracies to replace the previously anarchic corps of public employees. New York City's experience in organizing and controlling street cleaners and sanitation men is a case in point: "Colonel Waring found the Tammany employees despised by the public, having little respect for themselves and none for their work. Their positions were uncertain, as it was constantly necessary to make places for new men who needed reward. These men, without uniforms, without organization, one might almost say without obligation, succeeded in 1888, in cleaning 53 of the 342 miles of paved streets in the city district. Under Colonel Waring 433 miles of streets were cleaned from once to five times a day by an army of 2500 men, organized after military methods, taking as much interest in their work and as greatly respected by the public for it as are the members of the fire department. . . . These were the 'white wings' that never grew weary."[61]

By 1900 many cities had established publicly owned control over gas companies, waterworks, and transportation systems. In Warner's view, "all in all, the multiplication of public and private utilities was a major accomplishment of the 19th century city and one in which contemporaries took justifiable pride."

The Persistence of Urban Problems

Although they had made great advances in physical construction and institution building, city governments found that their problems and the need for policy solutions had just begun. Urban governments were able to build the physical and organizational infrastructure of the modern city, but they were unable to make that system work to solve or even cope with many persistent problems. Furthermore, city governments have largely failed to rebuild and adapt urban institutions in the face of both structural decay and changing problems.

The persistence of urban problems—both large and small—is easily demonstrated in the following examples.

Despite repeated reform crusades, corruption continues to be a stable characteristic of urban government. Scandals involving police corruption have broken out in New York City at regular intervals, leading to the creation of blue-ribbon investigating commissions in 1897, 1933, and 1970. John Gardiner and David Olson wrote in *Theft of the City:*

Municipal corruption can be traced back at least as far as the 1820's, when greedy local officials seeking instant prosperity for their crossroads hamlets were more than willing to sell out to promoters of rail and water transportation schemes. Steffens revealed similar rapacity in dealings between local governments and the mushrooming public utilities at the beginning of the twentieth century. Today, perhaps because most capital improvements have been completed or involve federal funding and thus federal auditing, local corruption seems to center on the enforcement of criminal laws and regulations and the awarding of government contracts, although suburbs and the rapidly growing metropolitan areas of the Midwest and Southwest still see the development of payoffs common in older cities fifty years ago.[62]

The authors' tour of municipal corruption—past and present—goes to Chicago, Newark, Jersey City, St. Louis, Reading, Pennsylvania, Los Angeles, Baltimore, and New York City. And it takes in ticket fixing, police corruption, kickbacks in engineering contracts, corruption in construction, organized crime, theft in the poverty program, election fraud, and various other "techniques of political graft."

Urban administrators have never found a satisfactory way to prevent outbreaks of violence between juvenile gangs.

They have never found a way to prevent residents from turning in malicious false alarms—almost at will. In the case of false alarms, urban administrators fifty years ago were experimenting with "a siren to attract attention to the firealarm box and provide for apprehension of the false alarmist. Another patent contains a camera which takes a snapshot of the individual setting off the alarm. The best idea, from the human-interest standpoint, includes a pair of handcuffs which manacle the 'culprit' the instant he sets off the fire alarm."[63]

Urban administrators have never figured out how to educate low-income children. Despite the myths that surround the old-fashioned city school system, recent research shows that the nineteenth-century school was experiencing the same failures that critics complain about today: "From 1890 on, so far as quantitative evidence allows us to document, the schools failed to perform up to their own claims or anywhere near the popular definition of their role. In virtually every study undertaken since that made of the Chicago schools in 1898, more children have failed in school than have succeeded, both in absolute and relative numbers. As schools expanded to match the growth of cities, so urban decay and school failure became virtually synonymous clarion calls among reformers and Jeremiahs alike."[64]

Urban policy makers have never found a way consistently to catch burglars and muggers in the act of committing their crimes. They have been perpetually unable to shut down the drug trade or drug addiction. As David Musto points out, during the last seventy-five years "responsible officials" have continually argued that between 50 and 75 percent of all crimes are caused by addicts.[65] (These estimates are almost certainly unreliable, but the perception that the drug problem persists is not.) In addition they have never been able to prevent family breakdown in poor neighborhoods, ensure that health and housing regulations are enforced, prevent high rates of welfare dependency among new immigrant groups (black or white), or prevent citizens from fearing crime far more than they experience it.

Urban Panaceas

In trying to cope with these persistent problems city governments have continually searched for and imagined that they have found many promising solutions. For example, the 1879 tenement house law, which required that there be an airshaft in the middle of the building, was viewed as a promising cure to the problem of slum housing.[66] And the development of "dumb-bell" housing was viewed as a great innovation. Today, of course, housing of this sort is viewed as among the worst slum housing in urban America. When kindergartens were first developed, they were viewed as a powerful tool for improving education. Indeed the advocates of kindergartens portrayed them as nothing less than a solution for urban education. In the 1960s head start programs were launched with high hopes of solving the educational problems that had not been solved by earlier solutions, including the kindergarten. The advocates of public playgrounds believed that most juvenile delinquency would be eliminated if youths had adequate recreational facilities. In 1910 one advocate of playgrounds asserted that 80 percent of 480 "juvenile delinquents" in one urban neighborhood might have been "saved" by recreation.[67]

Reactive Problem Solving and Erratic Search

The record of urban problem solving is perhaps most distinctive for its reactive character. Public health services grew up in reaction to frequent epidemics. The creation of public water systems was a response to disease and to the incidence of fires that all too often burned out of control. Organized sanitation departments were a response to health problems (as well as to the simple problem of population growth). In the same way organized police forces were a response to the realization that the night watch—with their rattles and their huts—were of limited use in handling nighttime crime and of no use at all in dealing with daytime crime. According to recent historical studies, public schools were in large measure at once a moralistic response to juvenile delinquency and vagrancy and a pragmatic response to the need to socialize large numbers of new immigrant children and prepare them for employment in an industrial society. Michael Katz has shown that public schools begin to regulate their instructional programs carefully in reaction to the "bewildering array of innovations being peddled around the country."[68]

The reactive nature of service delivery has another important feature. In trying to remedy particular problems or services urban administrators have tended to pursue the antithetical policy or mode of service delivery—and thus have fallen into the trap of what James David Barber calls mirror-image reasoning. That is, if decentralized, fragmented service institutions are seen to be inefficient and corrupt, the chosen remedy is centralization. If a later generation considers highly centralized institutions as the problem (because of their rigidity and lack of responsiveness), the chosen remedy is decentralization. The same dialetic exists in many other service areas, and it creates the same cycle in which services and policies bounce back and forth between opposite strategies. Thus in the nineteenth century reformers tried to solve problems created by home care of the mentally ill and community treatment of felons by creating special asylums designed to rehabilitate the sick and the criminal. Today urban administrators are trying to solve the problems produced by asylums by experimenting with home care and community treatment.

In the nineteenth century grading, tracking, and vocational programs were developed in schools to solve the perceived problems of rigidity and arbitrariness caused by teaching students of different ages and with different skills in a uniform way. Today educational policy is going the opposite way—attempting through the use of comprehensive schools, open classrooms, and other methods to correct the perceived problems of discrimination and stereotyping produced by highly differentiated schooling.

The evolution of urban policy has traced the same dialectical course we have encountered before between problem solution and problem creation. However, the fact that urban services and policies seem to be caught in this pendulum movement is not in itself evidence of governmental incompetence. The simple fact is that reliable answers do not exist for many of the city's most pressing problems, and, seen in this light, the erratic search for solutions that has characterized urban governance is perhaps easily understood.

The Changing Character of Urban Problems

The city of the 1960s presented urban policy makers and residents alike with problems that were significantly different and more difficult than those that city government confronted in the nineteenth-century city. The city that nonwhites encountered in the 1960s was no longer young, fast growing, and mounting large-scale services for the first time. Rather, cities like Boston, Philadelphia, St. Louis, Baltimore, Cleveland, Chicago, and New York were "aging". More concretely their service delivery systems were now fifty to one hundred years old (depending on the city and the service); their physical plants were deteriorating; and they were suffering an increasing rate of decay as a result. The key point is that although urban governments were relatively successful in laying out new services as the modern city grew, they have never been very successful in restoring or restructuring old services. In part this is because it is economically and technologically less costly to produce new goods and services than to rehabilitate them. Rehabilitation means eliminating outdated equipment or methods of operation and dealing with intricate interdependencies (between services or programs). Above all, it means challenging entrenched interests and disrupting established patterns of behavior.

For these reasons it was easier to build a service system in response to the demands of the immigrant era than it was to restructure and reform an established service system to meet the demands of new immigrants with different needs. Thus the institutionalization of services was an administrative triumph coming as a reaction to the nineteenth-century growth of the city. But in the 1960s the same phenomenon of institutionalization took on a very different significance: it was a source of persistence and inflexibility and therefore an obstacle to responsiveness and adaptation to new demands.

Most important, urban governments were grappling with a more difficult class of service problems in the 1960s than they had been in the preimmigrant era and during the periods when large-scale public works were being constructed. When government was merely supplying crude services like street paving and street lighting to urban residents, it was easily able to divide up service benefits and also to deliver the services effectively. Later when cities were building bridges, water and sewage systems, parks, and public transportation, the allocation problem was relatively easy for urban administrators who were dealing with indivisible public goods. There was little political conflict among individual urban residents or neighborhood groups over who was going to get a bridge or public water system. In addition, absent debilitating graft, cities had little trouble in actually constructing bridges, parks, and water supply systems. Finally in the immigrant era, the allocation of urban services was handled ingeniously (if not always equitably) by mutual adjustment between public employees and urban residents.

The services demanded in the 1960s, however, were intrinsically difficult to allocate and also difficult to deliver effectively. In contrast to earlier demands for either essentially private or essentially public goods, service demands in the 1960s centered on what might be called neighborhood goods. Residents of black and then white neighborhoods demanded that their communities receive better schools, health services, and police protection. More precisely, the dominant service demands were expressed in collective terms and remedy was sought not for isolated individuals or the city as a whole but rather for particular black neighborhoods and particular white, blue-collar neighborhoods. What this meant was that the service crisis could not be negotiated out on the basis of ad hoc individual exchanges as it had before. Nor could the crisis be resolved by providing public works that would benefit all urban residents. Poor, black neighborhoods in particular had no interest in new civic projects. What they wanted was improved social services in their areas. They knew too that these services had been allocated before to their detriment, and they wanted a larger and more equitable share of the benefits. In short urban policy makers were not being asked merely to distribute urban goods and services efficiently; they were under pressure from different blocks and neighborhoods to redistribute goods and services.

This conflict between neighborhoods for goods and services obviously constituted a deeply divisive force in urban government. Demands were made on city hall by people who said they represented the community—whatever racial, ethnic, or geographical community it was. In this context urban policy makers were forced to decide what constituted a neighborhood, what the relative needs of different neighborhoods were, and what constituted equity in service delivery. In addition since urban government now delivered many services that private organizations and markets had once provided (such as public welfare, many health services, and public housing), almost any service complaint could be politicized and turned into a controversy among city hall, the official bureaucracies, and the neighborhoods.

Finally the public perception of and definition of urban problems have changed substantially as the city's service delivery system has evolved. In the nineteenth century many social problems and, in particular, the problem of poverty, were blamed on the poor themselves. In 1845 the Association for Improving the Condition of the Poor admonished their volunteers: "The evils of improvidence can never be diminished except by removing the cause; and this can only be done by elevating the moral character of the poor, and by teaching them to depend upon themselves."[69]

This is only a more judicious statement of a citizen complaint in 1798 that public welfare supported "a worthless slum"—a "parcel of drones" who roamed the streets "in nastiness and filth" and preyed upon "the bowels of the commonwealth."[70]

In a similar view a central justification for the development of kindergartens was that they would teach the poor how to raise their children properly. In his study of the evolution of urban school systems, Michael Kaestle emphasizes the importance of moral training in education. The obvious implication is that the poor desperately needed moral training; and Kaestle provides the following account, written in 1840, of the perceived "moral" deficiencies of the poor:

In searching for children for *Public School* we witness scenes enough to shock human nature. In one family I obtained the promise of two children. They were to be in readiness the next morning at 9 o'clock. I called at that time. Her Mother had represented herself as a Widow but to my astonishment I met with the Father who had been let out from state Prison the day before—rather sooner than had been expected by the Wife—On his arrival he found her intoxicated, quite unable to attend to her Children and she was in the same condition when I called for the children. On my appearance a Scene commenced which cannot be described. Each tried to make the best story which was followed by blows and tumultous noise.—After waiting about 30 minutes I was compelled to leave with my mind made up that there are multitudes of children in this City who never will be benefited by Education unless they can be rescued from such an influence.[71]

Even the reformer Jacob Riis took the view that poverty was a "moral distemper":

How different this perception of the source of urban problems is from the more recently expressed views that social environment, economic inequality, racism, and "unresponsive" bureaucracies lie at the root of urban problems and poverty. For if the correct explanation of urban problems and poverty is found in the fundamental workings of the urban politico-economic system, then the assignment of responsibility is shifted drastically. For then it arguably becomes the job of government to correct its own failings and also to redress the injustices of race and economic distribution. If city government is held "morally" responsible for its citizens' problems, it is not hard to see why the legitimate demands on and expectations of government would escalate rapidly.[72]

The New Urban Politics: Twelve Patterns

In the 1950s urban government attracted little sustained attention from federal officials, newspapers and magazines, the public at large, or political scientists—so much so that in 1957 one political scientist, Lawrence Herson, was moved to write bleakly of the "lost world of municipal government."[73] The discovery of the urban crisis, the urban riots, the war on poverty, revenue sharing, and the thrust of impending municipal bankruptcy changed all that—at least in terms of public attention and anxiety. As a result various political analysts have begun to speak of a new urban politics, not to mention a new tradition of urban political analysis.

To this point we have considered both the distinctive characteristics of urban government and the evolution of urban problems and policies. But we have not addressed the question of whether there is anything new in the present structure of urban problems and policy making. Indeed the main purpose of my argument so far has been to illuminate fundamental and therefore persistent features of urban government, as well as historical patterns of political developments and institutional evolutions. Nevertheless it seems appropriate to speak of a "new" urban politics. What makes present city politics "new" is that the city of today contains several new features and patterns and several familiar ones that have been greatly intensified in the last decade or two. In the aggregate there is a difference of degree along many dimensions. Crucially the structural patterns that characterize this new urban system play a central role in the increased fragmentation, instability, and reactivism of urban policy making and thus contribute to making the city increasingly ungovernable. To summarize the argument, the shape of the so-called new urban politics can best be presented in terms of the following twelve features:

1. A sharp increase in the number of participants in urban policy making—bureaucrats, neighborhood groups, public service unions, higher-level governmentalists.
2. Greater conflict both within and between urban neighborhoods.
3. Greater racial conflicts within and between neighborhoods.

4. More programs and policies leading to a proliferation of functions performed by city government.

5. More issues and problems that are politicized and placed on the agenda of city government.

6. Greater bureaucratic fragmentation and conflict.

7. Greater conflict between citizens and public employees and a strong decline in social symmetry and mutual trust.

8. More intervention by higher-level governments and, as a result, greater fragmentation and conflict in the domain of intergovernmental policy making as it impinges on urban problems.

9. More problems—both persistent and emerging—that are social rather than physical in character and for which there are no agreed-upon solutions or demonstrated treatment technologies.

10. Greater expectation that city government will solve its major problems, linked with the public perception that city hall should be held responsible for the city's problems.

11. Far greater public consciousness of and concern about urban problems and crises.

12. Far greater pressures on the mayor, who must work in an increasingly unstable policy-making environment and deal with an increasingly chaotic agenda of urban problems.

4
The Structure of Urban Policy Making

The environment of policy making and the character of urban problems determine the shape of urban policy. Policy outcomes are a product of highly variable fragmented and unstable problem and policy contexts. And it is precisely because urban policy makers must deal with so many different, fragmented problem and policy contexts that urban policy making as a whole is so fragmented, unstable, and reactive. To understand more completely what urban policy making is about, let us consider a number of typical urban problems and policy contexts.

What should city hall do (if anything) about the recent rash of murders in one neighborhood, the tenant strike in another, or the unpopular principal, the harassment of firemen, the newly created and newly menacing youth gang, the protest against plans for a secondary sewage treatment facility, the new X-rated movie or massage parlor, the recently broken street light, water main, or catch basin, the garbage that has languished for a week on a particular block, the outbreak of fighting between white and black students in a recently redistricted high school, the discovery of corruption in the police department or in a municipal loan program, the vandalism of benches in a popular neighborhood park (or in school buildings), the outbreak of fires in an abandoned building, the suspicion that drug dealers have been hanging around a local school or that a large number of children in a neighborhood are suffering from lead poisoning, the discovery in a community that a hospital plans to expand down the block or that private developers intend to tear down a block of three-family homes in an old, stable neighborhood, or that a public union is close to calling a strike, and finally the allegation that police are beating up teenagers in a "tense" neighborhood. Which problem should the urban policy maker deal with first? Some of them are serious, some are routine. Some call for an emergency response, some do not. Some can be immediately verified, others are hard to identify. (In fact, in a large proportion of cases, it may be very difficult to find out exactly what is going on out at the street level.) Nevertheless, in every case some group of citizens will feel that their own problem is enormously important, that it is an emergency that must be dealt with immediately.

The first point to notice about this agenda is the length of the list. And before this list of problems can be sorted out, assessed, and dealt with (or ignored), a new list will have sprung up, demanding attention from the already overloaded central policy maker. The main implication of this demand structure is that central policy makers are forced to be reactive. They cannot easily plan for tomorrow's problems when they are fully occupied responding to today's, yesterday's, and last month's accumulated inventory. Given the constantly changing barrage of demands and problems central policy makers are likely to get caught in a frantic movement from one problem or issue to another. And if they set their agenda by responding to the most dramatic problems and the loudest complaints, they will be seen to be crisis hopping—caught in the process of rushing to the next fire. So the first point about street-fighting pluralism is that it puts urban policy makers in a highly reactive posture. The second main point is that the issues present so many different kinds of policy problems and evoke many different kinds of decision processes. Different problems and issues carry with them very different policy-making characteristics. The outcome of any given policy-making strategy is decisively shaped by the problem, issue context, institutional setting, stage of decision, configuration of participants, and government function involved. The implication is that the structure of the urban policy-making process will largely determine the content of public policy—whatever the nature of the power structure in a particular city.

Power Analysis Versus Policy-Making Analysis

My argument does not follow the contours of the community power debate; rather I ask how different demands and problems arise, how the government responds to them, what the main decision networks are in urban policy making, and how different problems and issues travel along them. The difference between a community power analysis and a policy-making analysis can be clearly seen by examining the case studies of decision making found in Robert Dahl's *Who Governs* and Banfield's *Political Influence* from the two different perspectives.[1]

Dahl looks at the structure of power and decision making in the areas of urban renewal, education, and party nominations. What interests him, given his concern to evaluate the power elite thesis, is that different actors (and configurations of actors) exercised power in the three cases. This suggests to Dahl that power and decision making are not monolithic in New Haven but rather pluralistic—characterized by an executive-centered coalition that revolves around Mayor Richard C. Lee.

Looking at these cases from a policy-making approach, the three cases involved such different problems and issues that they represented very different policy-making processes. Two of them, urban renewal and education, involved the delivery of public services—services that have a tangible impact on urban residents. But there were significant differences between the goods and services involved. The renewal meant large-scale capital construction that, as Dahl notes, initially seemed to offer something to everybody. In this sense renewal at first appeared to be a classic public good—a benefit to all members of the community because it promised to revitalize the city as a whole. For this reason citizen demands and interests were not at first sharply articulated or sharply conflicting. The mayor found that he had considerable room for maneuver in designing his renewal strategy. What is more, renewal was in an important sense a "free good"—paid for largely by the federal government and thus not requiring a reallocation of funds away from competing bureaucracies (such as schools and the police). Had it required such a transfer of funds, renewal would almost certainly have forced the mayor into a difficult bargaining process with his own government agencies rather than allowing him, as it turned out, to present renewal as a gift to the city. Further, the logic of urban renewal pointed toward central planning and administration. The federal government wanted to see a workable plan for the city's future development, and the very task of redesigning the central city called for a broad overview for a coordinated, central perspective. Also few, if any, cities had the administrative equipment in the 1950s to plan for and carry out renewal programs. Thus, in New Haven and elsewhere, mayors built redevelopment agencies as extensions of the mayor's office, and this only reinforced the centralizing pressures created by renewal. Renewal required expertise, long-range planning, and intricate (sometimes secret) negotiations with the federal government; it was a kind of policy making that an energetic mayor and his professional planners would naturally and easily dominate. Dahl indeed found that the executive-centered coalition was an overwhelming political success in renewal. In my view, however, this does not reveal nearly so much about the power structure as it does about the nature of the policy problem and decision process created by urban renewal.

In contrast to renewal, public education is an urban service that many citizens and administrators are continually involved in and care about deeply. Urban residents have long taken part in educational policy making through the central board of education, and local PTAs and various community groups, as well as the teachers' unions, regularly press their demands and interests on city government. In addition there is a long-standing, well-entrenched system of fragmented decision making in public education. The members of the board of education, the superintendent, the assistant superintendents, principals, supervisors, and the teachers themselves all figure into the policy-making process. For a mayor to imagine that he could centralize planning and administration in education, as he might well do in his own newly created redevelopment agency, would be foolish. (Aside from all the competing forces he would have to contend with, he would lack legal authority to give direct orders; the board of education has legal authority over the schools, and even in cities where the mayor appoints board members, there are many slips between political appointment and mayoral control of decision making.) Finally Mayor Lee and other mayors quickly discovered that the issues and problems facing the school system were very different and far more politically difficult than were policy problems in urban renewal—at least in its early days. Instead of dealing with the free public goods of renewal, mayors faced in education the divisive, sometimes explosive, issues of integration and busing, of unequal school facilities and expenditures. These were zero-sum issues, or so they seemed. There was no way to satisfy probusing forces without alienating antibusing forces. With these issues and the decision-making processes that existed in the schools, it is thus no surprise that, according to Dahl, no single power elite ran the New Haven schools or, for that matter, that Mayor Lee's executive-centered coalition did not operate in the sphere of educational policy making. Again, this analysis does not appear to reveal as much about the general power structure as it does about the character of urban policy making in a particular policy area.

Consider another example. In his *Political Influence* Edward Banfield presents a "new theory of urban politics" in which policy making is characterized by a "mixed-decision choice process." Put simply, this process is pluralistic in that it entails bargaining and compromise between several political institutions or actors. But the process also has elements of what Banfield calls "central decision." This centralized policy making lies in the active and powerful role that the governor, the mayor, and the county board play in Banfield's case studies of urban decision making. As he puts it, "There is, nevertheless, an important element of central decision in the Chicago system. The governor, the mayor, and the president of the county board are all in positions to assert the supremacy of 'public values' and, in general, to regulate the workings of the social-choice process."

Again, however, the conclusions about power relations are in large measure a reflection of the decisions Banfield chooses to examine, and to that extent his "new theory of urban politics" is an artifact of certain distinctive policy contexts and processes—which happen to generate a particular policy-making pattern (one which Banfield takes to be general).

What is so distinctive about Banfield's cases is that most of the cases were either about major city planning decisions in which both high-level city hall officials and major private sector (especially business) leaders were intimately involved, or they were about organizational conflicts between different levels of government. But they did not concern at all the daily conflicts in urban government about police, education, and other types of urban service delivery—conflicts that routinely involve myriad citizen groups and lower-level urban officials. In short these were not cases where the mayor had to deal primarily with conflicts between citizens and city government or internal conflicts between different institutions in his own government. Rather the cases captured city hall in what might be called "foreign relations" with private enterprise and with county and state governments. The cases were not insignificant for this reason, but they were quite distinctive. On the one hand the mayor lacked the power to try to control policy making directly. In such cases he could not order the state or the business community around. On the other hand he did not have to deal with the fragmentation of interests and demands that he found within his own government. Instead, in Banfield's cases, the mayor is dealing with other princes, the central decision makers in the state or the business community. And since the other players are independent and powerful, he deals through bargaining and compromise. The result is a "mixed decision-choice process"—in part centralized because it involves a small number of high-level leaders, in part pluralistic because competing independent institutions are involved and also because other interests have been expressed along the way. The point is that considering the context, issues, and actors involved, we would naturally expect the result that Banfield discovered. It is built into the policy-making process that operates in his cases.

In sum both Dahl and Banfield have tried to find the essence of urban power relations by looking at a series of case studies of decision making. But what they have really turned up is certain distinctive policy issues and contexts in which the policy-making process strongly determines power relations, not the reverse. If Banfield had looked at school policies in Chicago, we would expect him to talk more about fragmented decision making. If Dahl had looked at the conflicts between New Haven and the state of Connecticut, we would expect him to find Banfield's pattern of "mixed decision-choice." Clearly this analysis of Dahl's and Banfield's case studies suggests that the most profitable way to gain an understanding of policy making and the exercise of power in the city is to examine particular policy contexts and issues with a view to illuminating significant similarities and differences in the policy-making process.

A Model of Urban Policy Making

So far I have offered a verbal description of urban government as a policy-making system. To gain a clearer picture of the fragmentation, instability, and reactive character of urban policy-making, it is useful to present a metaphor of the city's decision processes based on three familiar games found in most penny arcades. First, we can think of the process of urban problem generation and agenda setting in terms of a shooting gallery—not the addict hangout (which is also an urban phenomenon) but the game in which a player (urban policy maker) is faced with a large number of moving targets —rows of ducks, pinwheels, and so forth. Like the urban policy maker the shooting gallery player has far more targets than he can possibly hit, and they keep popping up in different places or revolving around and around in front of him. The player is constantly reacting to a new target (problem) and at the same time is faced with the choice of which target (problem) to fire at (with the knowledge that firing at one target means letting the vast majority of others go past until the next time). Faced with this need to react quickly and to deal with such a bewildering array of targets (which, incidentally, have different payoffs), the player will frantically move from target to target—relying on reflexes rather than on any considered plan of action. There may be some extremely rational people (or expert marksmen) who manage to impose an orderly agenda of action on the shooting gallery game, for example, by shooting ducks in the top row first or by using all their shots on the pinwheels; but anyone who has played the game or observed it being played will probably agree that it is intrinsic to the structure of the game that the player is forced to be reactive and is likely to become frantic. So it is with urban agenda setting because of the structure of demands that arise from the city's street-fighting pluralism.

Second, we may think of the urban policy maker's ability to predict and control the decision games he must deal with in terms of the workings of a slot machine. Urban policy-making variables include the nature of the problem, the issue context, the stage of decision, the configuration of participants, the institutional setting, and the government function involved. The point of the metaphor is that the policy-making characteristics of an urban demand or problem can vary just as independently (randomly) as the apples, oranges, and cherries on a slot machine. For example, the first combination to turn up may be a resource problem in the context of health delivery in which a neighborhood group is pitted against a group of hospital administrators. This problem combination may call for the policy maker to hold a bargaining session and free up some extra budget lines from his budget director. Having followed this policy-making procedure, he may then encounter a second problem combination: a conflict over busing involving several neighborhoods, the board of education, and state and national government agencies. Clearly the first policy response is not appropriate to this case; the latter problem may require instead legal action, appeals to higher-level governments, and an immediate police response at the neighborhood level to prevent actual street fighting between black and white residents. Having adopted this policy response, the central policy maker may then face a third problem combination: a charge by several community groups that several principals in a school district are "unresponsive" or "insulting" and should be removed. In such a case the board of education may have its own independent or quasi-independent authority, and the teachers' union may threaten a strike if the city accedes to community demands. This kind of problem combination may plausibly call for crisis management—around-the-clock negotiating sessions—or perhaps the decision to implement a new plan for citizen participation and decentralization. Having responded in this way, the central policy maker may face a fourth problem combination: a complaint by the administrators in the welfare department that the city and state housing bureaucracies are refusing to help them arrange temporary shelter for welfare families who have been evicted from their apartments. Such a problem may call for the creation of a new interdepartmental task force or the development of a new state-local policy agreement (to be negotiated directly with the governor). But the appropriate policy response bears little resemblance to the responses called for by earlier problems. Finally, consider a fifth problem combination: two policemen, along with several journalists, tell the policy maker that there is widespread corruption in the police force and that the internal police watchdogs are either ignoring the problems or covering them up.

The point of the slot machine metaphor is that the central policy maker never knows what kind of problem he will be dealing with from moment to moment and also does not know which of his available policy responses or procedures will be relevant or useful. This underscores the point that urban policy making is highly unstable. A policy maker who wishes to rely on one or two standard responses, or to develop a standing plan for decision making, will find that he has guessed wrong much (or most) of the time. Imagine a central policy maker who relies exclusively on any one of the following policy-making guidelines: (1) systematically analyze the benefits and costs of different policy alternatives; (2) bargain and compromise with the principal combatants; (3) appeal to state or national governments for more money; (4) create new mechanisms for citizen participation; (5) create new coordinating committees or planning task forces within city government; (6) stall or put off the decision (in the hope that many problems will go away); (7) adopt a moralistic, crusading posture, including symbolic expressions of commitment or opposition to a particular policy; (8) assign blame for problems to rigid bureaucracies, stingy higher-level governments, the economy, suburbs, white racists, militant blacks, and so forth.

Few actual policy makers would tenaciously cling to any one of these strategies to the exclusion of all others. But the point is that because of the "slot machine" character of urban decision games, a rational policy maker who wished to tailor his policy response to each different problem would be constantly forced to change his procedures and strategies and would never know which one would be called for next. This is what I mean by the fundamental instability of urban policy making.

Third, we can think of the process of implementation in urban policy making in terms of the operation of another familiar penny arcade game: the pinball machine. Given the central policy maker's weak control over his own administration, street-level bureaucrats, and higher-level governments, decisions once taken are likely to bounce around from decision point to decision point.[2]

The implication is that even when a decision is made on a policy devised in city hall, it will be knocked off course by both known and unforeseen obstacles by the time it reaches the street level. If this is true, the implemented policy is likely to raise a new set of problems and demands that will enter into the shooting gallery of agenda setting all over again. To that extent urban policy making will become a continuous process in which a particular problem receives brief, often frantic, attention; some kind of decision is made, which bounces around in the implementation process; and then the problem pops up again in a new or slightly altered form. This means that problems are not dealt with in a steady and sustained fashion but rather are fired at erratically. Thus policy making on any one problem or set of problems is unlikely to develop in a linear fashion or in small closely related incremental steps. Rather the development of a policy is likely to trace an unstable, uneven course: either zigzags, circles, or possibly unrelated targets. To this extent urban policy making will have a distinctly evolutionary character: urban problems and policies will continually change—in a protean fashion. Consider the following examples: a strict code enforcement program leads to housing abandonment, which requires a new set of policy responses; urban bureaucracies are centralized and professionalized to overcome the perceived defects of decentralization, but it is not long before demands for decentralization arise in response to the perceived defects of centralization; policies toward drug addicts, criminals, and juvenile delinquents veer back and forth between community treatment and institutionalization with each strategy offered as a solution to the problems caused by the other; public concern over prostitution, massage parlors, and other issues of public morality erupts sporadically in one neighborhood or another and then quickly dies down; youth gangs come and go, sometimes viewed as a menace and other times as a possible instrument of community development, sometimes providing protection against outsiders and other times running protection rackets; an old neighborhood evolves from a working-class neighborhood to a black slum to a high rent area populated by the upper middle class within a decade; the drug problem rapidly shifts from heroin to cocaine to pills to alcohol and back to heroin; the police department moves to car patrol

to increase coverage and visibility and begins to receive community demands that patrolmen be put back on the beat in the interests
of responsiveness and visibility. In the face of these problems, the
question is validly asked: What is a mayor (or other policy maker)
to do?

Rational Decision, Incrementalism, and Reactive Policy Making

The penny arcade model presents a stark metaphor of the uncertainty, instability, and reactiveness of urban policy making. Indeed
it somewhat exaggerates the randomness of urban policy-making
games, for there are certain emerging patterns in the structure of
urban problems and demands that reveal a great deal about the
character of the new urban politics. Nevertheless the penny arcade
model serves to distinguish sharply the city's policy-making system
from the national system as it is depicted in the two most influential
models of policy making.

The first theory, which is really a vision of how policy should
ideally be made, is that of rational, comprehensive decision making. According to this view policy problems should be approached
and solved through a systematic, rigorous analysis of goals and
means, costs and benefits. This theory of public decision underlay
the introduction of systems analysis in the defense department under Secretary Robert McNamara, and the development of program
planning budgeting systems (PPBS) throughout the federal government during the Johnson administration. According to the rational analysis approach to problem solving, the policy maker is
imagined to play an active and highly intellectual role. He identifies
the policy problem and lays it out for careful inspection. In a sense
he freezes it for further study as a scientist would freeze a laborato-
ry specimen. He then examines alternative ways of dealing with the
problem and attempts to measure (or estimate) the likely impacts
of alternative policies. The goal of policy analysis is to find the best
solution for the problem at hand. Having found the answer, the
policy maker designs an appropriate new policy and implements it.
Taken as a whole, rational decision making has a distinctly scientific look to it: the policy maker relies on his ability to gain thorough
knowledge about particular problems (and the relationship be-

tween them) and on his mental capabilities to separate issues and make precise calculations about utility and efficiency. Throughout it is assumed that answers can be found for policy problems if enough intelligence is brought to bear on them. A further assumption is that the analytically best or most efficient solution is also the best solution for practical policy in a political world.

This rational, synoptic method of problem solving may seem a sensible way to reach an intelligent decision on many sorts of policy issues. We would expect no less from public works engineers, defense department contractors, architects of housing projects, and scientists involved with power plants and pollution control. The rational model of decision making, however, does not adequately describe the policy-making process in urban government; instead it constitutes an inappropriate, unworkable strategy for much of urban policy making because, from the urban world of street-fighting pluralism, it is too formal, precise, abstract, and tidy. It is a greenhouse conception that cannot thrive in the harsh climate of urban politics. In the first place the rational decision maker is supposed to pick his problem and analyze it with detachment and great care. Instead urban policy makers are constantly reacting to new or changing service demands and policy problems. They find it very difficult to stop the policy-making process, freeze a particular problem, and then dissect it in a clinical fashion. More important, they routinely deal with problems whose nature and solutions they either simply do not understand or only dimly understand. They cannot find the answer to police corruption, street crime, or educational failures through research and analysis. Rather they grope for a plausible remedy and see if it will work any better than previous ones. In addition service demands typically raise questions of reactive deprivation (does x neighborhood need more services than neighborhood y?) and thus of political pressure and political priorities. Such issues do not call in the first place for analytical solutions but rather for subjective assessments and for political bargaining and adjustment.

Further the rational decision model fails to take account of the fact that urban policy problems change and evolve so rapidly. In this context to abstract and analyze a problem in a meticulous, detached way may be to lose track of the problem and wind up fighting yesterday's battles. Also the fact that the administration of decisions in city government is so fragmented and even chaotic means that the question of what is the right decision is basically moot unless the question of how the decision can be effectiveiy carried out is answered.

The theory of incrementalism, as developed by C. E. Lindblom, also does not provide a satisfactory understanding of urban policy making.[3] Incrementalism implies a relatively stable policy-making process in national government, which is held in equilibrium by the constant adjustment (or mutual adjustment) of many different interests. It further entails a gradual, steady development of programs and policies. Any particular policy decision is built on a sturdy foundation of prior decisions (which have shaped the content and direction of policy), and the new decision extends or changes the existing line of policy only incrementally. Even when incrementalism is disjointed, when many different people deal separately with different policy questions, the policy process is held together by bargaining—the "hidden hand in government."[4] With its fragmentation, instability, reactivism, and erratic or blind search for policy solutions, urban policy making simply does not resemble the intricately balanced policy process of incrementalism. More precisely even though both the incremental model and the penny arcade model allow for a large number of players, the players in the former case play the same game (that is, are willing to play the bargaining game), whereas the players in urban government find themselves in highly dissimilar games (depending on the problem combination) and are by no means always willing to trade and negotiate in the interests of mutual partisan adjustment. Rather urban players often find themselves in stalemates, confrontations, and nondecision games in which opposed players do not bargain or adjust at all because each has a separate piece of authority or policy jurisdiction and can therefore operate in feudal isolation from competing players and baronies.[5] In short the many players in the incremental model find established, predictable channels and mechanisms for working out their bargains; in the model of urban policy making the players enter into an unstructured, unpredictable policy process: the free-for-all of street-fighting pluralism. As a last point of contrast, there are simply not as many players per decision game in incrementalism as in the urban system of street-fighting pluralism. In Lindblom's and Wildavsky's accounts the main players are the familiar ones in the national system: presidents, bureaucratic agencies, congressional committees, and interest groups; in the urban system the players run the gamut from individual residents to community organizations, to policemen, to city departments, to mayors, to higher-level governments.[6] The central difference between the models of national decision, incrementalism, and reactive policy making is shown in figure 1.

Finally the three models differ dramatically in the kinds of search processes they produce in decision making. In the rational decision model the dominant search process involves a search for knowledge and efficient policy in bargains. But in the reactive policy-making model of city government, the search process is more difficult to specify. It is clearly not a consistent, controlled search. Rather it would seem to be an erratic search process when policy makers veer back and forth between available (and often opposed) strategies. And it is a blind search process when, in the extreme cases of uncertainty and instability, urban policy makers are looking for any solution.

The Elements of Urban Decision Making

I have stressed the uncertainty and instability of urban policy making. The slot machine metaphor in particular suggests that the basic elements of urban decision games can vary almost randomly, creating constantly changing problem combinations that call for very different policy responses. The next step of this analysis is to flesh out this rather abstract analytical model by examining each of the elements of decision making in some detail. The basic elements of urban decision include the nature of the problem, the issue context, the stage of decision, the configuration of participants, the institutional setting, and the government function involved.

An examination of these basic elements will show more clearly the actual stuffing of urban decision games and reveal emerging patterns in decision making. My argument is that although deci-

Figure 1. Instability, uncertainty, and number of participants as properties of policy-making models

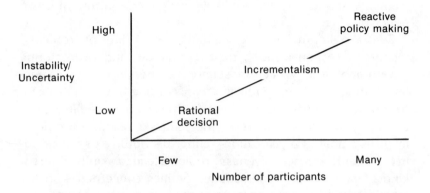

sion games will always vary in a bewildering way, there are significant trends and consistencies in the character of the different elements of decision that are likely to shape the future of urban policy making.

Central policy makers face five fundamental kinds of problems: resources, responsiveness, trust, regulation, and restructuring government itself. What is most important here is that the character of urban policy making will vary according to which problem (resource, responsiveness, and so forth) is emphasized in a given decision game. More concretely the politics of resource problems involves a politics of allocation—either distributive or redistributive. By contrast responsiveness problems lead to a quite different kind of politics: an administrative politics concerned with the architecture of service bureaucracies. For example recent government strategies for dealing with responsiveness problems have led to the creation of little city halls, neighborhood service centers, the appointment of ombudsmen, and the delegation of increased decision-making power to neighborhood-level service administrators. Trust problems also lead directly into the tangle of administrative politics, with the emphasis placed again on street-level strategies. These have included community relations programs, minority recruitment efforts, and civilian review boards. To reiterate, the central political task arising from trust problems is how to alter the administration of service delivery to bridge the social, psychological, and often racial gaps between the servers and the served.

Regulation problems also lead to an administrative politics in which central policy makers argue with one another about the best way to tighten up, monitor, or evaluate the work of urban bureaucracies. The main difference between the politics of regulation problems and the politics of responsiveness and trust problems is that the former imply a centralization of power and control. For example, in trying to deal with regulation problems city governments have created departments of investigation, special prosecutors, central policy planning offices, project management programs, productivity programs, and various other devices for improved management and evaluation.

Finally restructuring problems lead to a very different kind of politics, involving city governments in both bargaining games with outside players (suburbs, higher-level governments) and renegotiations of local authority relationships (as in the case of plans for community control).

There are several emerging trends in the incidence and salience of the different problem types. First, resource problems will always be central, but, for two separate reasons, decisions about new expenditures and resource strategies are likely to engage the energy and imagination of urban policy makers far less than they did in the 1960s. In the wake of its frustrating experience with the war on poverty, the federal government has moved away from innovative public spending programs that tend to focus urban policy making on new resource strategies. Further, given the austerity budgets of city government, the resource problem is taking on a different character. Instead of leading to decisions about how to allocate new expenditures, contemporary resource decisions require all players to lose something or force the city government to redistribute existing resources from one bureaucracy or neighborhood to another. In this context resource problems impose strong constraints and political costs on urban policy makers rather than providing opportunities and political benefits.

Second, problems of trust, responsiveness, and restructuring are emerging as the most critical urban problems. Regulation problems are always present and tend to erupt from time to time when charges of corruption or racism or brutality are made against one urban bureaucracy or another. Trust and responsiveness problems, which are the fundamental problems of street-level service delivery, have become dominant in recent years because of the perception that urban spending programs are simply not being implemented at the street level and because racial tension and polarization have greatly increased the mistrust between street-level bureaucrats and an increasing percentage of urban residents. These are the kinds of problems that push urban policy making in the direction of decentralization strategies and citizen participation.

Restructuring problems also have a decentralizing thrust to the extent that they involve demands for neighborhood government. And to this extent, responsiveness, trust, and restructuring problems all come together in their focus on the need to reform the street-level service relationship. However, restructuring problems are increasingly pulling in a different direction: toward an emphasis in policy making on the city's relationship with other governments. The problem here is how to reform intergovernmental relations on all levels to provide planning and equitable financing in the future in policy areas such as education, health, welfare, environmental protection, and urban growth. Thus urban policy making is simultaneously being pulled in opposite directions: to a concern with the street-level service arrangements on the one hand and to a concern with the structure of intergovernmental planning and policy making on the other.

Issue Contexts

A major source of the instability of urban decision games is that the demands arising from the city's street-fighting pluralism present so many different issue contexts. The main variables that distinguish different issue contexts follow.

1. *Private versus collective goods* The most familiar urban services take the form of private goods—highly divisible goods that can be delivered in different quality and quantity to different people and for which different people typically have different private needs. Indeed street-fighting pluralism grows out of the fragmentation of a citizen demand structure oriented to these private goods. However, other kinds of public goods are provided by city government. For example, in the era of city building in the nineteenth century, urban governments supplied public goods that benefited the entire population of a city collectively. Among these citywide public goods were the development of city water supply systems, the draining of mosquito swamps to prevent disease, the construction of bridges, and, to a lesser extent, the development of central parks. More recently other kinds of collective goods have appeared on the urban agenda and have produced new and difficult issue contexts. One kind of new collective good might be called a "neighborhood good"—for example, a particular zoning, busing, housing, or highway routing decision that vitally affects

the interests of a neighborhood. A second kind of new collective good is one that involves the interests of residents in a metropolitan area, a state, or a multistate region. For example, decisions concerning environmental protection, energy allocation, economic development, and educational financing typically impinge on the collective interests of these larger communities. Thus the distinction between private and collective goods is not a dichotomous one; rather it involves a continuum, which can be expressed as follows:

Private   Collective
Goods   Individual→ Neighborhood→ Citywide→ Metropolitan→ Statewide→ Regional   Goods

The point of this analysis is straightforward. It is difficult enough for urban policy makers to deal with the demands for private goods that give rise to street-fighting pluralism; it is even more difficult for urban policy makers to deal with demands based on the supposed interests of neighborhoods and larger-scale communities. In the first place conflicts between neighborhood interests pose controversial issues of redistribution and preferential treatment. Does the urban policy maker favor poor neighborhoods, working-class neighborhoods, or affluent neighborhoods? The very language involved in describing these issue contexts suggests the political difficulties involved. Issues relating to the interests of even larger communities impose a different kind of burden on urban policy making: they lead to relations with other governments and thus to a policy-making process in which city government has even less control over policy outcomes than it does on issues that arise entirely within city limits. Thus urban issues increasingly involve neighborhood and larger-scale issues; to this extent, urban policy making has become increasingly difficult.

Different private, neighborhood, and citywide goods not only make for differences in the difficulty of policy making; they also shape and strain the institutional structure of urban policy making in different ways. Consider the implications of a demand for a neighborhood good, in institutional terms, as against a demand for a citywide or metropolitan good. The first sort of demand creates significant centrifugal pressures on government—because of the nature of the issues involved—whereas the second, more collective demand, creates centralizing pressures on the structure of government.

When urban policy makers confront demands for street-level or neighborhood goods, they will react by moving to decentralized government—at least on the issue involved. The experience with community action and school decentralization illustrates this point. Conversely when policy makers confront demands for citywide or regional goods, they will move to build or strengthen centralized institutions.

Different policy issues thus pull the governmental system in different directions, and urban policy makers thus are under constant pressure to redesign governmental institutions in light of the character of policy issues salient at a given time. The final point is that demands for private goods are the easiest kind for city hall to manage. This is because ad hoc, fragmented demands for services can be dealt with by a reactive, fragmented government. Indeed meeting highly particular service demands is what the city does best.

2. *Benefits and costs* Issue contexts also differ according to the benefits and costs involved for different participants. In general the easiest ones to deal with are those that distribute many benefits to urban residents and impose little or no cost. Such issues are also rare. Next best for urban policy makers are issue contexts in which particularistic benefits are given to certain people or groups without cost to others. Historically many service delivery issues have been of this character as city government has acted to take care of a pothole here, a broken water main there. But with the increased awareness of citizens about their private and neighborhood service needs, it is now more difficult for urban policy makers to take care of service demands on a piecemeal basis. Urban government is perceived as making deliberate choices about which pothole to fill, and residents with unfilled potholes are likely to conclude that their demands have been slighted or ignored.

Consider too the cost side of urban issue contexts. It is logical to believe that decisions that impose concentrated costs on particular neighborhoods will be difficult ones to implement because they will be strongly resisted. Resistance will be particularly fierce if the decisions involved produce strong but scattered benefits. The difficulty of dealing with issues involving concentrated costs and dispersed benefits is evident in many recent urban controversies: neighborhood renewal projects, scatter-site housing, busing programs, the siting of methadone clinics, sewage treatment plants, and prison halfway houses. Thus the rise of self-conscious neighborhood interests greatly increases the liklihood that any single issue will be seen to impose concentrated costs and therefore will be highly problematic for urban policy makers.

An analysis of recent urban case studies confirms the thesis that the structure of benefits and costs produced by a given issue powerfully shapes the resulting policy-making process. Consider first an issue that involves a public good that affects most urban residents but carries only relatively small and invisible benefits and costs for any one person or group. In this case the issue probably will not be hotly contested or will not achieve a prominent position on the agenda of city government. This is precisely what Matthew Crenson found in his study of urban policy making on air pollution, *The Unpolitics of Air Pollution.*[7] Crenson tries to explain this pattern of "nondecision making" in terms of industrial influence, the fragmentation of decision making caused by the city's pluralistic politics, and the difficulty of raising new and unsettling issues (including the "public interest" issue) when many different actors are fighting to protect their own interests. I agree in general with the importance of the last two factors and have no reason to dispute the first, but I believe we can find a simpler explanation of the unpolitics of air pollution in a cost-benefit analysis of the issue. As long as air pollution does not impose heavy and visible costs (both health and environmental costs) on the public, it is likely that there will be no strong public notice or coalition determined to do something about the air. Rather, urban residents will remain concerned with those issues that affect their daily lives directly and tangibly. In addition, in terms of the logic of collective action, it will be difficult to mobilize any group to protest against air pollution unless the group is confident that the larger affected public is dissatisfied with air conditions and is ready and eager to join in the protest.

The utility of cost-benefit analysis is evident if we compare Crenson's study of air pollution in Gary and East Chicago with policy making on similar public issues in which the cost-benefit structure is somewhat altered. The closest point of comparison with Crenson's study is the treatment of the issue in Los Angeles where the costs of pollution have become severe and visible. In contrast to Crenson's unpolitics, air pollution in Los Angeles has become a salient and persistent issue on the agenda of city government. As another point of comparison, in the cities Crenson studied intensively, Gary and East Chicago, dirty air carried substantial benefits —at least indirectly—in the sense that it meant that local factories were running and employing local residents. In any cost-benefit calculation the air pollution issue will be viewed differently in Pittsburgh and Honolulu.

The logic and impact of different cost-benefit structures are perhaps even clearer in the case of water supply politics and policy in New York City where the adequacy of the city's water supply is not much of an issue. But if a severe drought should cause an acute water shortage in the summer, the water policy issue can quickly become controversial and contested because the nature of the cost structure is fundamentally altered. Instead of being an issue that affects most people very slightly, water supply becomes a public good that affects all urban residents directly and tangibly. This is exactly what happened in New York City in 1965 when the city's water shortage became the predominant issue in the Democratic mayoral primary. Instead of revealing a pattern of unpolitics, the question of water supply produced a very lively and even slightly hysterical public controversy.

So far I have argued that the salience and persistence of an urban issue will depend on the structure of the costs and benefits that are imposed on urban residents. More precisely the cost-benefit structure of an issue can be usefully analyzed in terms of the number of people affected, the magnitude of the costs and benefits for any given people or group, and the tangibility and visibility of costs and benefits. The strength of the cost-benefit analysis of urban issues is that it provides simple, nonconspiratorial explanations of why certain ones burn brightly and why others fail to create any sustained public attention. In particular when the costs of an issue are geographically concentrated, the issue is likely to gather steam rapidly, but when the costs are dispersed, it will be difficult to develop support for it.

Consider the case of lead poisoning. Activists have bitterly accused urban policy makers and the press of insensitivity to the problems of poor children suffering from lead poisoning. But if we consider the cost structure of lead poisoning and its implications for political mobilization, we can easily see why attention to this issue tends to be so slight and erratic. The trouble with lead poisoning as an urban issue is that it imposes dispersed and often invisible costs on urban residents. (The fact that the costs of lead poisoning are borne by children, who are a silent political constituency, reinforces the low salience of the issue.) In the first place the costs of lead poisoning are often invisible, even to the parents of the affected children, because the disease does not produce any acute symptoms in its early stages. Second, the costs of lead poisoning are not sharply concentrated among a particular group of urban residents. This is because lead poisoning has an erratic and uncertain impact across a large population of low-income residents living in old houses. There will be a few lead cases in one building on one block, but the other cases are apt to be dispersed irregularly through the neighborhood.

The key point is that lead poisoning simply does not affect any one block or small neighborhood as tangibly and visibly as plans for urban renewal or highways or the expansion of a hospital or the location of a drug treatment center. Generally when proposed urban policies impose concentrated costs on small geographical areas, the opposition is strong and persistent, and the issue tends to produce emotional public controversy. This pattern was found in Jewel Bellush and Stephen David's account of scatter-site housing in New York City where the invaded neighborhood managed to turn the scatter-site policy into a public furor and, in so doing, soundly defeated integrationist forces throughout the city.[8]

In sum, to the extent that an increasing number of urban policies impose or are seen to impose concentrated costs on small neighborhoods, policy making is increasingly constrained, and the political costs of urban governance are greatly increased.

3. *Symbolic versus material issues* The classic problems of urban service delivery have always been tangible, specific, material— things that needed to be fixed, requests for an additional school or number of policemen. The demands that arise from these prob-

lems can therefore be clearly met. Both the servers and the served could easily tell when the service problem had been taken care of. Recently, however, as a result of the greater political self-consciousness of urban residents, urban issues have frequently been defined in highly symbolic terms. Problems are often described not in terms of the specific service complaint but in terms of inequality or a lack of sensitivity on the part of public employees or "institutional racism." In addition issues are now being defined symbolically that were never defined at all when urban policy making was focused on material service problems. Recent controversial urban issues have referred to quality education, neighborhood development or decay, and alienation from government. Because these concepts are symbolic and hard to pin down, it becomes that much more difficult for urban policy makers to define the problem and devise a way of responding to it (assuming that they want to in the first place). Symbolic issues tend to be angry, polarizing, emotional. They often involve fighting words. Once articulated, they are inherently hard to control and resolve.

Issues tend to become highly symbolic when they involve racial conflict and disputed social welfare policies in the city. Equally important, some issues become highly symbolic and hard to manage precisely because they have come to be defined as racial issues by political adversaries in the course of public debate. Finally polarizing political symbols often are attached to far more ordinary urban issues either when they are deliberately put forward as crises by involved interest groups or when they reenact a persistent urban morality play in which the citizen is pitted against city government.

The racial symbolism that grew up around the civilian review board in New York City was highly devisive. As Bellush and David have shown, the idea for a civilian review board arose as a way of assuring minority groups that their complaints about police conduct would be heard by city government.[9] It was thus an attempt to increase responsiveness in government and trust between city hall and nonwhite neighborhoods. The Police Benevolent Association, along with a number of conservative groups, opposed the board as an unwarranted interference in police department affairs and an attempt to undercut police authority. The opponents succeeded in getting the issue put to referendum vote, and at that point the racial symbolism surrounding the issue grew in force and divisiveness. The minority group advocates of the review board increasingly dwelled on the issue of police brutality, which carried the clear implication that the police were racist. In turn the opponents of the board emphasized "crime in the streets." And in case the racial symbolism of street crime was not clear, the PBA underlined the symbolic point in their advertising: "A much publicized advertisement showed a young white woman emerging from the subway, alone and apprehensive on a dark street. The caption read: 'The Civilian Review Board must be stopped! Her life . . . your life . . . may depend on it.'"[10]

Social welfare policies tend to produce emotional symbolic issues because urban residents hold strong and sharply divided views about these policies but know relatively little about the social conditions that they attempt to deal with. This is a perfect environment for an angry and destructive form of symbolic politics. As Diana Gordon has shown in one of her New York City case studies, public discussion of emergency housing for welfare families produced a polarizing symbolic issue that was used as a powerful political weapon by both advocates and opponents of welfare programs. The problem of housing welfare families in New York recurrently erupted into a highly symbolic crisis issue, only to recede from the public agenda when the angry charges and countercharges subsided. Recently the issue was that the city was spending large amounts of money to house welfare families in decaying welfare hotels, and, when there was not enough room there, in expensive motels (in one case the Waldorf Astoria). The use of the Waldorf was in itself a symbolic act by a frustrated social worker to dramatize the plight of the welfare families. However, the issue hardly needed any further symbolic dramatizing. According to Gordon's account,

. . . contributing to the public furor over the hotels was the fact that they were being supported—to the tune of $40,000 a month to the Hamilton Hotel, and over $18,000 a week to the Manhattan Towers—with "taxpayers'" money. This news produced two kinds of reaction. Many were horrified that such vast sums should be spent on such "hell holes"; they tended to be sympathetic to the hotel families and critical of the City bureaucracies that had placed and kept them there. Others, in a reaction that was predominant in the 1947 situation, focused their ire on the people for whom the money was being spent. They saw the families in hotels as lazy and undeserving, living off the hard-earned dollars of the middle class.[11]

The point is that the rise and fall of this symbolic issue contributed nothing to urban policy making. The problem was not addressed in a sustained way, and almost no enduring policy changes were made. City officials were too busy reacting to the public furor.

4. *Independent versus intertwined issues* Historically the most familiar service issues also had the characteristic of being relatively independent of one another. The task of building a school in one neighborhood had nothing to do with the task of policing the street or fixing a pothole. Separable issues of this sort present clear advantages to urban policy makers for they can be rather easily sorted out, assigned, and monitored. In contrast to these simple urban issues, those that confront policy makers in the new urban politics are increasingly intertwined, so it is hard for even the careful policy analyst to figure out where one dimension of the issue begins and another ends. Such issues involve not only multiple problems but also impinge on the work of several different urban bureaucracies. A good example of an intertwined issue is lead poisoning, or street crime (as related to drug addiction), or educational problems (as plausibly related to health, housing, and nutrition problems), or problems of discipline and crime in schools (which are at once problems for teachers, policemen, and often social workers). Because urban issues are increasingly intertwined, it is more difficult for urban policy makers to cut into a problem and develop a policy response. Hence they are faced with the difficulty of choosing which facet of an issue to attack and of trying to figure out whether they can treat just one part of it.

In her account of the controversy over lead poisoning in New York Diana Gordon shows how the fact that the problem involved issues of housing, health, public education, and medical testing fragmented policy making and frustrated both a clear definition and a sustained policy initiative.[12] In addition, Gordon's study of New York's welfare hotels also illustrates this point. The intertwined problems of welfare policy, housing policy, and government regulation and inspection (of the welfare hotels) led to a policy-making fiasco in which city departments wound up blaming each other for the welfare hotel problem, ignoring the fact that the problem arose in the first place because the departments had not worked together on a joint problem.[13]

5. *The means-end relationship* Many traditional problems of urban service delivery were also clearly solvable. City governments knew how to build shcools, hire policemen, and pave streets. Having, in fact, solved many of the most easily solvable (and often technical) urban problems, city governments now find themselves left with an increasing proportion of issues where they literally do not know how to solve the problem (even if they wanted to). This leaves urban policy makers in the new urban politics in the awkward position of focusing on precisely those problems that they have been least able to deal with in the past.

Urban policy makers have made significant and sustained advances in public health, physical construction, and service organization where there are both clear technologies and significant continuing technological improvements. But where there is no established technology (increasingly the case with the difficult urban problems) and where there are many competing street-level interests (as is normally the case with all urban problems), no stable or demonstrable means-end relationship in problem solving is likely to exist. In this context the search for policy will take the form of a blind search—a spasmodic, diffuse search for some strategy that looks promising and might be effective. Historically policy making in education has provided the clearest and most enduring example of a blind search for a viable program or policy. In the last hundred years educational policy makers have tried out (and often reinvented) a great number of new ideas: compulsory attendance, graded classrooms (as against one-room classrooms), tracking systems, moral education (and citizenship training), manual education, playgrounds and recreational programs, kindergartens, standardized testing, affective education, centralized management, nonpartisan boards of education, head start programs, desegregation and busing, open classrooms, community schools, decentralizing community control, the nurturing of black consciousness and pride, paraprofessionals, performance contracting, voucher schemes, teaching machines, team teaching, bilingual education, planned experimentation, and so forth.

In recent years, the pattern of blind search, produced by a feeble means-end relationship in problem solving, has been most sharply manifest in police efforts to combat street crime and in efforts to treat and prevent drug addiction. Consider the case of drug policy as it developed in New York City during the Lindsay administration. Diana Gordon put it this way: "As Lindsay looked at the murky problem of drug abuse in New York, he could think only that he needed to do something and to do it fast and visibly. In a sea of ambivalent experts, one person stood out who might be able to shoulder the burdens to provide some answers: Efran Ramirez."[14] Ramirez termed his treatment strategy "existential psychiatry"—involving the creation of therapeutic communities designed to force addicts to face the "requirements and challenges of reality."[15] After receiving reports that this approach seemed to be working in Puerto Rico, Lindsay named Ramirez as his first narcotics coordinator.

Reaching out blindly Lindsay embraced the first hopeful idea he encountered, and it is not at all obvious that he had any better search process at his disposal. However schisms soon arose within Ramirez's community of addiction service administrators, and rival programs arose. In time the city turned from therapy to chemistry and decided to emphasize methadone treatment programs.

By the time Graham Finney became commissioner of New York's Addiction Services Agency in 1970, he found that as a result of the blind search process, a bewildering number of experiments were in operation, but there was no way of knowing what impact, if any, the experiments were having. To find out what was going on in his drug treatment domain, Finney called an all-day hearing at city hall. Each treatment and prevention program was allotted ten minutes to describe its approach and any measure of its success. Nearly 150 agencies were summoned.[16]

6. *Problem definition* The most familiar and traditional urban service problems—problems of cleaning the streets, filling potholes, putting out fires, and building new schools and hospitals—had the characteristic of being easily and unambiguously defined. The

business of delivering old-fashioned urban services to individuals could be managed because the problems were obvious and plausible solutions could be applied.

By contrast in the world of street-fighting pluralism many groups and interests fight over issues that are increasingly intertwined and symbolic, that involve concentrated costs and demands for neighborhood goods, and that have no easy (or known) solution. In this context it is often very difficult to define the nature and boundaries of present-day urban problems. The consequences of weak and ambiguous problem definition are straightforward. In the first place a problem cannot be solved (or any plausible solution attempted) if the problem has not been clearly defined. Second, to the extent that the process of problem definition itself becomes the subject of many-sided arguments and conflicts, the policy-making process will become even more unstable (since problem definitions may change rapidly) and also fragmented (since different urban policy makers may act on the basis of different and conflicting definitions of the problem).

Recent urban case studies provide many examples of the instability and fragmentation of problem definition in urban policy making. For example, Alan Altshuler's study of the Ancker Hospital site controversy deals with a planning decision in St. Paul that concerned alternative proposals for improving or replacing the hospital's "outmoded" and "uneconomical" facilities.[17] At first the problem seemed to be defined in economic terms: what was the cheapest way to buy an adequate hospital facility? But soon very different definitions of the problem were articulated, and these competing definitions complicated the policy-making process.

A second definition of the problem was offered by doctors and planning consultants who believed that the issue at stake was whether St. Paul would gain a medical center as a result of the decision on Ancker Hospital. They believed that if a new Ancker facility was built near St. Paul's two largest private hospitals, sufficient medical resources would exist to provide the foundation for a major metropolitan medical center.

Yet another definition of the problem was offered by businessmen in the vicinity of the old hospital. In their view the problem was one of neighborhood preservation, and they believed that if the hospital were moved out of the area, the neighborhood would go into rapid decline.

A further definition was articulated by a planner in the Housing and Redevelopment Authority who argued that the problem at issue was one of rational redevelopment strategy in the city and urged that the new hospital be built in the eastern redevelopment area where the city already had available land and where there was almost unlimited room for expansion, landscaping, cheap surface parking, and living facilities for the staff.

The final definition was by far the most divisive, for it turned the planning decision into a religious issue: the location of Ancker Hospital next to the city's two other hospitals would mean a mixing of public and religious institutions. This definition became a major feature in the decision when St. Paul's official organization of Lutheran ministers resolved that the proposal for a combined medical center would violate the constitutional insistence on the separation of church and state. What started out as an apparently straightforward planning issue, centered on economic costs and benefits, became in large measure a many-sided fight over the definition of the problem.

The Stage of Decision

A third element that adds to the variability and instability of urban policy making is the stage of decision. In the simplest terms the problem that pops up on the city's slot machine of pressing issues may be a new one that no one has ever encountered before or an old familiar one that the city now deals with routinely and effectively. Or it may be an entirely different kind of old problem—one on which numerous constraining decisions have been made in the past and for which decision making is now deeply constrained by existing policies, programs, and expenditures. Thus the city may be locked into its treatment of the old problem, and any new approach would require a basic restructuring (or rewiring) both of policy and of existing administrative organization. Urban policy makers will often deal with problems that are at still other stages of decision. For example, some problems (such as drug addiction or prostitution) may regularly arise, force some response, and then appear shortly in a slightly different form. These are also recurrent problems that are treated each time they appear as a new crisis issue: a serious water shortage or a public union strike or a fiscal crisis or a rash of murders or rapes in a neighborhood.

In terms of crisis issues and crisis hopping there are very different stages of decisions. In the first stage of crisis decision the mayor may make some quick statement or literally rush to a fire (or disaster) and then move on rapidly to the next crisis. Here the mayor's reaction is similar to what Mayhew calls "position taking": He gets himself on the public record but does not take any particular action.

If the crisis does not go away after the mayor has paid momentary attention to it, he will move rapidly to provide some new program or policy (or reverse an existing one). For example, he might try to prevent demolition of an old building that a neighborhood has been fighting to preserve, or he might order police into the schools to deal with a sudden increase in vandalism, theft, and fighting. In this stage of crisis decision the mayor feels compelled to do something about the problem, but because of pressures to act quickly about other crises and noncrises, the mayor typically reacts by reaching for a quick solution in the hope that the problem will be reduced by his brief spasm of action and attention.

In the third and most protracted stage of crisis decision, the mayor faces a crisis that simply will not go away and that drives all other problems and decisions off the city's agenda. The mayor cannot continue to rely on his standard crisis reactions: making a public pronouncement or appearance (position taking) or quickly developing a new program or policy (the quick solution). Rather the problem requires more sustained attention; it may be a citywide strike that cuts off a vital service, a riot (or series of riots) that turns racial conflict into actual street fighting, or a fiscal crisis that requires the firing of city employees and cutbacks in city services.

Curiously this is the only kind of urban crisis decision that resembles crisic decision making in foreign policy, where policy makers work around the clock to come up with a response to a clear emergency. The emergency decision places heavy burdens on urban policy makers because it physically exhausts them and places heavy psychological stress on them to act decisively in the face of unusually great risk and uncertainty. There is no doubt that a mayor who had to deal with one emergency decision after another would find the city increasingly ungovernable, but it is usually the succession of small, variable crises coming from so many directions and involving so many different participants that makes the city so difficult to govern. Constant, small-scale crisis hopping fragments city hall's attention and makes its policy making reactive and erratic.

In more general terms let us consider what difference the various stages of decision make for a central policy maker. A central policy maker who wished to control (manage) his city as easily as possible would clearly prefer to deal with problems that he is familiar with and has learned how to treat routinely (as against problems that are either new or that require a restructuring of government); and he would prefer to deal with relatively small issues as opposed to relatively large ones. But in the new urban politics city hall policy makers not only are forced to deal with a more difficult range of issues, but they also encounter these issues at stages of decision that are more difficult to manage and control. The basic distinctions developed above are presented in figure 2. This analysis suggests that the best (most manageable) decisions are found at and around point B, which represents decisions that the policy maker is familiar with and knows how to respond to. In this context policy making involves either relatively small adjustments in policy and program or incremental allocations of existing services. This is the kind of policy making that traditionally occurs when city hall responds to tangible service requests such as a demand to fix a pothole or repair a traffic light.

In the new urban politics, however, city hall policy makers must increasingly deal with issues at points A, C, D, E, all of which exist at a distance from point B where decisions involve only small adjustments and allocations. In particular, urban issues cluster at point A, the point of constant crisis hopping, and at point E, the stage of evolutionary decision making, and both of these stages carry high costs for decision making.

Figure 2. Stages of decision

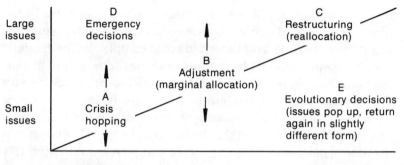

Configuration of Participants

If the central urban policy maker could control his political environment, he would doubtless choose to deal with street-level demands one at a time, and he would avoid complicated multilateral decision games that involve various city bureaucracies and higher-level governments. When the central policy maker has to trade off the claims of different neighborhood groups, he inevitably winds up in the position of disappointing as many interests as he pleases. And the greater the extent that he has to participate in multilateral decision games with other agencies and governments, the less likely he is to be able to respond quickly and flexibly to any single demand.

The simple point is that urban issue contexts increasingly involve a multiplicity of participants. This is in part because of the proliferation of neighborhood-based interests, in part because of the intertwined character of urban issues (drawing in different bureaucracies), and in part because of the increased involvement of other levels of government in urban issues. My empirical proposition is that in modern urban politics, policy makers will be increasingly faced with multilateral decision games that include community groups, city bureaucracies, and higher-level governments. This multiplicity of participants imposes high transaction costs and makes it all the more difficult for city government to make coherent decisions—or for that matter any decisions at all.

Conclusion: The Politics of Urban Policy Making

If the central policy maker is a political actor who wishes to be liked by constituents and to stay in office and who can best gain support by taking credit for solving citizen problems, the new urban politics makes his job very difficult. He does not even have to be a perfect rational economic man to realize that he is best off dealing with private goods that confer particularistic benefits (and avoid concentrated costs) and that are not symbolic in character, intricately intertwined, and unsolvable (given his present knowledge and resources). Further he would like to avoid multilateral decision games so that he can respond as he sees fit, and he would like to have bureaucracies working for him that are accessible to citizen concerns and that are capable of controlling the implementation of their services. Thus on every count the central policy maker is likely to be disappointed and is apt to become involved in decision games that disadvantage him systematically as both a problem solver and a politician.

To put this analysis into a broader structural context, the central policy maker is required by the new urban politics to deal with two quite dissimilar problems. He is asked at once to work out a more effective street-level service relationship that meets the twin problems of trust and responsiveness and at the same time to bargain effectively with other governments on the growing number of issues that extend beyond city limits. On both counts he is in severe trouble, and this is one reason for the suspicion that urban government has become increasingly ungovernable.

5
Dynamics of Decision: The View from City Hall

Although the main elements of urban decision combine unpredictably to create many different decision games and therefore give urban policy making its fragmented, unstable, and reactive character, there are also certain key shared characteristics of urban decisions. There are common patterns in the way urban decisions develop and, in particular, common patterns that explain what makes one kind of decision game more difficult to handle than another. The task of this chapter is to introduce the main dynamic forces in urban decision—the forces that impinge on any decision and whose magnitude in a decision determines the relative ease or difficulty of that decision. The characteristic features of the new urban politics create decision dynamics that are intrinsically hard to control and that make city government increasingly ungovernable.

We can see more concretely what the dynamics of urban decision making look like in city hall and what makes some decisions harder than others by considering a number of decision games that I have observed at close range in New York City. My argument is that a central urban policy maker will have increased difficulty governing the city to the extent that (1) decision games involve larger numbers of participants; (2) the participants represent institutions, such as the board of education or state government, that the central policy maker does not directly control; (3) the demands made by the participants are diametrically opposed and thus lead to zero-sum decisions; and (4) the decisions involve highly charged political symbols. Thus the greater the number of participants and/or the more that participants are not controlled by city hall, the more likely it is that demands will require zero-sum decisions, and the more likely, too, that symbolic politics of a highly polarizing nature will arise.

The Manhattan Bus Route

A relatively simple decision game developed in New York in 1966 when a city-owned bus company decided to change its bus routes in Manhattan.[1] The change was intended to streamline bus routes and simplify scheduling, but it had the further effect of increasing the walking distance to the nearest bus stop for residents in several

neighborhoods in the city. Residents in two of these neighborhoods, Greenwich Village and West End Avenue, complained
bitterly to city hall. Local politicians and leaders of community
organizations gathered testimony from neighborhoods about how
far they now had to walk to the bus stop and how long they had to
wait. They also prepared a movie showing West End Avenue residents trekking to the new bus stop and waiting in the rain during
rush hour. Finally they rounded up twenty or thirty area residents
and descended on city hall for the board of estimate meeting at
which the route changes would be reviewed by city officials. This
decision game provided an opportunity for the mayor to listen to
(and be seen to listen to) community grievances and, as it turned
out, to make a decision that was responsive—that satisfied neighborhood grievances by making a minor adjustment in the new bus
routes. The only cost of the mayor's decision fell on the city
bureaucracy, which was now forced to revise its plans (although
the plan as a whole was implemented).

The key to the decision game is that the mayor was able to look
effective politically—and to provide concrete benefits for a well-
organized neighborhood—without incurring any substantial costs
in community conflict or in conflict within his own bureaucracies.
The issue was tangible and concrete, and the mayor had the clear
ability to solve the problem. Neighborhood interests were specific
and, most important, the decision did not involve a zero-sum
game. The mayor was able to improve the position of the Greenwich Village and West End Avenue residents without making any
other community worse off. The political benefits of adjusting the
bus routes substantially outweighed the costs, and, as a result, the
central decision maker was able to make a quick decision. The bus
route case is one that any mayor would like to deal with all the time.

The Washington Square Library

In the summer of 1966 a neighborhood conflict arose in Greenwich
Village that involved the mayor and his assistants in a more difficult
decision game.[2] The conflict grew out of New York University's
plans to construct a new library on a site adjoining Washington
Square Park. The university, which at the time had no central li-

brary facility, contended that the proposed library was desperately needed—that NYU could not develop as a distinguished educational institution or even maintain its present stature if it did not have adequate library facilities. The university noted with pride that the library was being designed by a renowned architect and would make an important architectural contribution to both the neighborhood and the city. In their most ebullient moments university administrators and the architect liked to say that the addition of a library on the southeast corner of the park, along with planned future construction on the east side, would give the park a symmetry and elegance of design comparable to the Place Vendôme in Paris. For NYU the library promised to provide both a centerpiece for the campus and a symbol of increasing academic distinction.

The local residents were not moved by NYU's expression of its needs or by the architect's vision of Parisian elegance. The leaders of various community groups, who had joined together to stop the library, believed the building would destroy their park. They argued that the construction of a six-story building would ruin the character of the square, which still had many fine, old, low-rise buildings around it. According to neighborhood critics, the library would block sunlight to the park, hamper pedestrian movement around the square, and create a railroad station effect (because so many students would be using it, hanging around outside it, and eating their lunches on nearby park benches). Neighborhood residents also complained that the library plans were fraudulent (the building was actually going to contain plush offices for university administrators), the university had not consulted with neighborhood residents about the plan (except at a pro forma cocktail party), and the library was just the opening wedge in a program of university expansion that would eventually destroy the neighborhood.

In dealing with this decision, the mayor and his assistants first attempted to sort out the various issues and points of conflict. The mayor met with both university and neighborhood groups at city hall and heard the cases for and against the library in some detail. It quickly became apparent that there was little room to negotiate. The university was committed to the site adjoining the square, and the neighborhood representatives insisted that they had so many different, significant objections to the library that even if one or two objections were effectively challenged, their case was still persuasive. For this reason the mayor's effort to assess the factual premises underlying the dispute was of little use. For example, when the city established that the proposed building actually was going to be a library (and not an administrative palace), the neighborhood residents merely shifted their attack to a different objection. When it was also established that the library would not cut down substantially on sunlight in the park, the residents used their aesthetic and architectural criticisms and complained that the library would create a railroad station effect in that corner of the park.

It was soon clear that the mayor had no choice but to decide for one interest and against the other. As the residents put it in an early meeting, "The question, Mr. Mayor, is whether you are for us or against us on this issue." Added to the difficulty of this zero-sum decision, the mayor wound up in the position of being asked to choose between two powerful political values and symbols: the excellence of educational institutions in the city or the preservation and integrity of neighborhoods. City hall policy makers obviously wanted to identify with both symbols; unfortunately they were forced to vote against one.

In the end city hall decided to support the construction of the library, for which they were praised by NYU and condemned by Village residents. In terms of political costs and benefits the Mayor gained support in the nonprofit sector (but few votes) and lost support in a neighborhood whose votes were thought to be very important for any liberal, reform politician running in the city. When this decision game was over, the deputy mayor noted that if a mayor had to make fifty such zero-sum decisions, his support would erode to the point that he would no longer be a viable political leader. He would have made too many enemies.

The 1966 Transit Strike

On the day that John Lindsay took office in 1966, the city's transit union went out on strike, interrupting service for five million riders. The day before the leader of the Transit Workers Union, Mike Quill, had rejected the first offer made by the transit authority, terming it a "peanut package." In Quill's view the mayor was arrogant and intransigent, and he predicted that it would be a long strike. Lindsay was no less outspoken about his view of the conflict and the source of the problem. He told reporters at a news conference that the city "will not capitulate to the lawless demands of a single power group."[3] He added that New York was being victimized by a group of power brokers who were seeking private gain at the expense of the city and its citizens. At first glance this decision game appeared to be a straight fight between city hall and a major public union—albeit a fight involving another zero-sum game in which a victory for one side was necessarily a defeat for the other. In fact the transit strike was complicated by the involvement of several other players: the independent three-member Transit Authority, a mediation board, and the courts, which considered the Transit Authority's antistrike injunction and eventually jailed sixteen union leaders for defiance of a court order.

For the mayor and his city hall policy makers this decision game proved to be considerably more difficult and costly than the two previous cases. The strike ended after almost two weeks when the union accepted the mediation panel's proposals for a two-year, 15 percent pay rise and other benefits. In addition to these clear economic costs, city hall paid other heavy costs—both economic and political—in the course of the strike. The Transit Authority estimated that the city lost over $300,000 a day during the strike from a loss of revenues. The strike and the settlement also increased the operating deficit of the Transit Authority and forced the city both to raise the fifteen-cent fare (which had become something of a sacred cow) and to beg the state government for more aid. Further the mayor could only look on with distress as the union leadership first marched off to jail as labor martyrs and then proudly announced that the settlement was a smashing victory for the union.

What made this decision game difficult was that it presented a sharply defined zero-sum game that neither side was willing to lose. It was also a zero-sum game with large external effects, for it presented city hall with a choice between two very costly alternatives. To give in to the union demands at the outset would have increased the economic problems of the city and set a precedent for other public unions. To endure a strike would place economic costs on the city as a whole and make city hall appear incapable of dealing with its labor problems. Thus, whatever strategy the mayor pursued, he would incur severe external costs beyond the direct costs of whatever wage settlement that was eventually reached. In this sense the transit strike was more difficult and costly for urban policy makers than the zero-sum conflict over the Washington Square library.

Second, a strike affecting six million riders immediately became a citywide political issue. Newspapers and the public at large quickly registered their grievances and preferred solutions. By contrast the two other decision games did not become citywide political controversies, and the conflicts that they presented were to this extent easier to limit and deal with.

As with the NYU library the transit strike shows how easily urban conflicts are transformed into highly symbolic controversies between political opponents. In the transit strike Mayor Lindsay first pushed the conflict onto a symbolic plane by defining it as one between the power brokers—shadowy, sinister, but unnamed villains—and the public interest. Not to be outdone, Mike Quill retorted that the conflict was really between the upper-class elite represented by Lindsay and the little guy, represented by the transit workers seeking a decent wage. The decision game shows that with some wit and imagination, anyone can play symbolic politics and thus raise conflicts over particular interests into political crusades of one sort or another.

The School Strike

In April 1967 following the city school board's initiative, the state legislature mandated the mayor to produce a decentralization plan by December 1. Mayor Lindsay appointed McGeorge Bundy of the Ford Foundation to draw up a plan for the city. In July the city school board formally approved the formation of three experimental demonstration districts and the Ford Foundation provided $135,000 in planning grants.

Thereafter one experimental district, Ocean Hill-Brownsville, moved rapidly to bring about community control in its neighborhood. Indeed by August Ocean Hill had held elections for parent members of the first demonstration board. According to Barbara Carter the Ocean Hill community threatened to close the local school if neighborhood groups were not given the right to choose its principal.[4] The board of education reacted to this threat by creating the new post of demonstration principal, hoping that this semantic maneuver would satisfy both the teachers who opposed a neighborhood-picked principal and the community who wished to pick its own candidate and that a serious administrative and symbolic problem would fade away. But the problem immediately arose when the Ocean Hill neighborhood announced that it was considering appointing as demonstration principal Herman Ferguson, "a black militant accused of plotting to murder Whitney Young, Jr., and Roy Wilkins."[5]

By September 1967 the conflict was beginning to escalate rapidly. Schools opened with a fourteen-day teachers' strike over wages, class size, and teachers' powers. In the course of the strike Ocean Hill parents picketed the striking teachers, and, as soon as the strike ended, union teachers began to leave the Ocean Hill district in large numbers.

By November Bundy had presented a sweeping decentralization plan, and the Principal's Associations, joined by the United Federation of Teachers, had brought suit against the post of demonstration principal. In this period the mayor was working in the background to get the major antagonists talking to one another and to put a new decentralization plan into operation. But he was severely limited in his ability to make direct decisions himself or to compel either the board of education or the community to follow his wishes.

Given the number of participants, the decision game soon came to be played out on a number of different but interacting levels —rather like Chinese checkers. In January 1968 the city board and the three demonstration districts became engaged in the struggle over the powers assigned to the neighborhoods. The central board wished to suggest guidelines for neighborhood power, but the districts rejected the guidelines and demanded a list of specific powers. At another level the state supreme court ruled in March that Ocean Hill's principals had been illegally appointed. And at a third level various factions in the state legislature offered their own plans for school decentralization and wrangled over the central question of how much power should devolve to community boards. The state legislature was not working in isolation either. When it was reported in May that the legislature was leaning toward a strong decentralization bill, Albert Shanker (the head of the teachers' union) and five hundred teachers descended on Albany, and support for the bill soon collapsed.

The burgeoning conflict in the schools erupted into what the main participants considered a crisis when in May the Ocean Hill board fired nineteen white principals and teachers, announcing that their services were terminated and ordering them back to central headquarters. Subsequently neighborhood groups refused to let the disputed teachers into the school, and local union teachers in Ocean Hill-Brownsville walked out in protest.

By the end of May the Ocean Hill board had agreed to allow some of the disputed teachers back into the school but not back into the classrooms. The teachers' reaction was to walk out again; 350 teachers left the school and stayed out for the rest of the term. By this point the city's now familiar process of reactive policy making was clearly in motion, and the street fight became citywide and increasingly bitter.

In reaction to the second teacher walkout, Ocean Hill terminated the contracts of the 350 teachers. Then the city school board presented an interim plan, giving local boards limited power to hire and fire. In response Shanker promised a citywide strike if the plan was implemented. The courts dismissed the community's charge against the disputed teachers for lack of evidence and ordered Ocean Hill to take them back. The response of the city board was to adopt an even stronger interim plan "permitting local boards to transfer teachers among consenting districts." The teachers' reaction was immediate. The union went out on what was to be the first of three citywide strikes.

The first strike ended quickly, but a week later, on September 13, the teachers went out on a second strike when Ocean Hill once more refused to take the fired teachers back. The second strike was ended when Ocean Hill was ordered once again to comply with the court order.

In October after several community demonstrations, the local board reacted sharply to the outside pressures being placed on it and relieved the fired teachers of their assignments for the third time. At this point the decision process was out of control, and the mayor was forced to realize that his attempts at mediation had completely failed. In rapid order the board of education removed the local board and its principals, and a school in the district exploded into actual street fighting between community residents and teachers. According to one report:

The situation fell apart completely. Albert Van, assistant principal at 271, a head of the African-American Teachers Association, led a demonstration march of teachers and pupils out of 271 and off towards IS 55 and other schools in the district, picking up parents and demonstrators along the way. Crowds clashed with the police. Eggs and bottles flew. Nine were arrested. Scores were injured, including ten policemen. At one school, a mob burst into the teachers' room just as they were having lunch. "Get out, get out," they yelled. "We don't want you here." JHS 271 was hurriedly closed and so were other schools.[6]

In response to these events the teachers voted to strike for the third time. The strike kept more than a million students out of school for over a month and was resolved only when the Ocean Hill district was placed under state trusteeship and three of its demonstration principals were removed.

The school decentralization case provides a textbook example of an intractable decision game because all the elements of decision that, from the mayor's vantage point, make the city ungovernable, were present in exaggerated form. In the first place the game involved many different players: the mayor, the board of education, the teachers' union, the courts, the state legislature, the neighborhood school board, the newspapers, various community groups, and the Ford Foundation. Second, and even more important, the principal actors were relatively independent of the mayor's authority and influence. The mayor was thus constantly frustrated in his attempts to nurture communication and compromise between the board of education, the local board, and the teachers' union. As one aide recalled, the mayor spent most of his time carrying messages between groups and then discovering either that the messages had changed or that one side was misinterpreting what the other was trying to say.[7] Third, the decentralization issue presented several zero-sum conflicts: between the central and local boards over authority in the schools and between the union and the local board over the rights of teachers.

Fourth, and most important, the school strike shows how readily multisided conflicts develop into fierce symbolic battles and how destructive these symbolic battles are for the city. The decentralization confrontation began as an administrative reform that had ostensible support on all sides. Indeed in the late 1960s decentralization was an idea whose time appeared to have come, and it seemed to offer advantages, if not solutions, to players on all sides.[8] But the administrative issue raised by decentralization was almost immediately transformed into polarizing symbolic issues. In the conflict between the board of education and the local board, a disagreement about the right to transfer teachers was transformed into a fight over the nature and distribution of authority in the city and was played out as a confrontation between the system and the people. More damaging still the debate between the union and the community rapidly devolved into charges of white racism and black racism. Thus the teachers picketed with signs that read "community control means racist control," and community residents marched with signs that read "student strike against racist teachers."[9] Black community leaders perceived the teachers' opposition as evidence of colonial, racist attitudes, and teachers interpreted the firings and certain statements by black militants as clear evidence of virulent anti-Semitism. In the end the decision game dissolved into an argument about who was oppressing or persecuting whom. As such it was totally impervious to politics or policy making as usual. Once the conflict began, it is difficult to see what the mayor could possibly have done to prevent it from running its deeply destructive course. Nor is it easy even for a Monday morning quarterback working six years later to think of strategies that would have worked well for the mayor at the time.

Contestants and Symbolic Politics

My analysis of these decision games in New York City demonstrates the way in which the configuration of participants shapes the outcome of policy making. The basic proposition—that the difficulty of governing the city increases with the number of participants—is in fact firmly supported by other urban research. In their study of fluoridation decisions Robert Crain and his coauthors found that the more people there were involved in a decision, the fewer the chances were that fluroridation would be adopted.[10] They concluded that "broad popular participation, particularly in the absence of strong executive leadership and an institutionalized channel for the expression of opposition, spells defeat to fluoridation."[11] The fluoridation study shows that the participative society is problematic—makes governance more difficult—when political leaders do not or are unable to play a guiding role. And this is exactly the policy-making role that mayors inhabit much of the time in big city politics.

The second proposition, which is a corollary to the first, is that decision games will become more difficult for the mayor to deal with the more that major participants are independent of city hall. Because of the fragmentation of urban politics, most participants have some independence; some, however, have a formal, institutionalized independence and authority. In this sense the board of education (if it is formally independent) poses a considerable difficulty for city hall policy making, and a state or federal bureaucracy poses the greatest difficulty. This proposition is strongly supported by Edward Banfield's analysis of decision making in Chicago. Banfield concluded that "as the number of autonomous actors in a situation increases, the probability (that a new proposal will be adopted) decreases. This is so because there is some probability that an autonomous actor will choose to withhold a requisite action." Further, "as the number of autonomous actors increases, control tends to become less structured. Structures of control, relationships which are stable from proposal to proposal, are expensive to maintain. The value of a structure—and, thus the amount that will be invested in it—tends to decline as the outcome of the process becomes less and less subject to control."[12]

The third proposition—that decision games become more difficult the more zero-sum conflicts are involved and that zero-sum conflicts increase with the number of participants—appears at first glance to be a simple matter of probabilities. Imagine that there are three possible relationships between players in a decision game and that the relationships occur with equal frequency. The first relationship is one of compatibility between the claims of two players (both players roughly want the same thing). The second relationship is one of possible compromise (the players can strike a bargain that makes both better off). And the third relationship is one of direct opposition (if the first player gains x benefit in a decision, the second player loses by the same amount). In a simple world where each outcome arises with equal frequency, a decision game with three players would produce one zero-sum conflict, a game with six participants would produce two zero-sum conflicts, and a game with nine participants, three zero-sum conflicts. It should be obvious that a decision game in which there are three irreconcilable conflicts of interests is more difficult to work out than one with none or one. The difficulty is a simple function of the range and intensity of the conflicts involved. And, unhappily for mayors, the worst conflict patterns arise in the urban world of street-fighting pluralism.

So far the logic of urban decision seems quite straightforward. But symbolic issues greatly complicate the dynamics of urban decision games because they are polarizing, pitting one player against another in an intense way. The result is that when highly symbolic issues arise, zero-sum conflict will also arise with greater frequency, and urban decision making will become more difficult and even intractable.

Notice the crucial point: the likelihood that decision games will become highly symbolic increases with the number of participants. Thus we must explain not only why symbolic conflicts are so widespread in urban decision making but also why they increase in frequency when the number of participants in the game increases.

There are several reasons why symbolic issues arise so frequently in urban policy making. First, because of the fragmentation of urban government and the many cleavages both within and between urban neighborhoods, players in urban decision games are apt to have little personal familiarity with their adversaries. And being unknown to one another they tend to perceive their opponents in simple stereotypes. The mayor's assistant becomes "city hall," the school administrator becomes the "board of education," and the representative of a particular neighborhood group becomes "the community." When this labeling process occurs, we are well on our way to having a symbolic game in which abstractions like the community, the city, and old-line bureaucrats are seen to be doing battle. Most important, many people come to view these mythic conflicts as substantive and real.

Thus there are symbolic battles between "the neighborhoods" and "elite institutions" rather than specific, bounded conflicts between, for example, New York University and Greenwich Village organizations over the construction of a proposed college library. It stands to reason too that when the decision game is defined in these terms, the conflict will naturally escalate because so much more appears to be at stake than the original issue might have implied. The crucial point for the city is that as long as its policy making is characterized by fragmentation and street-fighting pluralism —in short, by a large number of players and constantly changing decision games—it is likely that the different players will remain largely unknown to one another. If this is so, the likelihood is great that a labeling process, which produces polarizing symbols and stereotypes, will persist.

The mayor will probably also have great difficulty in gaining personal familiarity with the majority of players in the decisions he must deal with. Unable to learn the individual traits of particular union members, union leaders, neighborhood leaders, business leaders, or bureaucratic officials, he is likely to perceive an urban world filled with various phantoms: power brokers, militant neighborhood leaders, business, the unions, the press, civil servants, the community, the federal government, ethnics, and so forth. A big city mayor is doubtless drawn to this kind of symbolic labeling as a way of ordering a complex world, but it is not a strategy that encourages carefully differentiated perceptions of competing interests or, for that reason, subtle bargaining and compromise.

The tendency toward polarizing symbols is reinforced at the neighborhood level by the decline of social symmetry between citizens and street-level bureaucrats. To the extent that the social distance between neighborhood residents and public employees increases in the city personal familiarity between the servers and the served obviously decreases. With that loss the problem of establishing communication between government and neighborhood intensifies. As a result each party to the service relationship is increasingly likely to view the other in the now familiar polarizing symbolic terms. To take an extreme case, residents, no longer having any personal relationship with a "cop on the beat," will often talk about their problems with the police or the "pigs." Policemen, in turn, do not perceive themselves to be dealing with particular merchants, teenagers, housewives, or landlords but rather with a "hostile" community or the "Spanish community" or adolescent males. By contrast the business of higher-level governments is very much based on stable and personal contacts and relationships. At least this is the prevailing wisdom in accounts of state and national government. In state and national legislatures lobbyists are said to be effective precisely because they have worked out personal relationships with legislators. Even more important, policy making in national government is heavily shaped by stable, personal relationships that grow up between members of congressional committees and bureaucrats in federal agencies. But in city government, where the central business relationship is between the servers and the served, the business of government is conducted not so much by old associates or cronies but by strangers who often view each other as enemies.

A second explanation of the propensity of urban politics to produce harsh symbolic conflicts lies in the nature of the resources available to the various participants. Many urban players, and particularly community groups, lack basic political resources that make for a strong bargaining position in a decision game. Community groups typically have little formal power, scant economic resources, and little expertise in dealing with government. As a result they might reasonably conclude that they would be overwhelmed in a straight fight with city hall and the bureaucracy who possess (or who are believed to have) well-established resources: formal authority, administrative experience and expertise, and time (especially time for delay). The community group can then try to improve its bargaining position by invoking dramatic political symbols. Thus it (as well as other urban players) may employ symbolic issues, such as community control, institutional racism, and police brutality, as a way of gaining leverage against opponents whose existing resources they cannot match. They seek to add a new dimension to the decision game: the dimension of symbolic politics on which they have a comparative advantage over more entrenched players in city hall and the bureaucracies who normally would like to contain conflict and avoid shouting matches and unseemly brawls with community groups. Looking back at the New York City decision games, we can see this use of political symbols by the Greenwich Village opponents of the New York University library (in protesting the destruction of their neighborhood) and by the Ocean Hill-Brownsville leaders (in raising their conflict over community control into an issue of white racism and power to the people).

Third, because of the overloaded, unstable character of the urban agenda and the tendency toward crisis hopping in city hall, neighborhood groups may reasonably conclude that the only way to get an issue on the agenda is to somehow make their own issue into a first-rate crisis. Even if the issue is not a clear and present crisis that must be attended to immediately, the group can make it so by dramatizing it, enveloping it in highly charged symbols. Recall two earlier examples. If it proves difficult to interest city officials in the general problem of lead poisoning in the city, a series of newspaper articles focusing on the death of a young child may work (that happened in New York City).[13] The point about symbolic politics is that death from lead poisoning was not the fundamental policy problem; it was rather that many children might be incurring a variety of significant but not fatal disabilities. But the story about a single case of death from lead poisoning did have the symbolic, dramatic force to arouse widespread concern. Similarly if social workers are not able to get city hall to pay attention to the problem of placing displaced welfare families in welfare hotels, lodging a welfare family in the Waldorf Astoria may have the symbolic force to make city hall react to the more general problem.[14] The policy problem was not that welfare families were being housed in large numbers in the Waldorf. But a single, well-dramatized case had the effect of creating immediate outrage and demands that city hall ameliorate the problem. At this point it should be obvious that the propensity of the press to emphasize the most dramatic urban problems only strengthens this use of symbolic issues, for local newspapers have proven to be better able than most officials or citizens to get a mayor to react quickly to an issue. In this context the city hall reaction begins when the mayor finds a microphone stuck in his face and a reporter asking, "What are you doing about the welfare family in the Waldorf?"

Fourth, with the fragmentation of street-level interests and demands even within relatively small neighborhoods, symbolic issues can play the crucial role of defining and mobilizing a neighborhood or a group that previously was split into many separate factions. The residents of Greenwich Village may not have been united on the architectural, aesthetic, and environmental issues supposedly posed by the New York University library. Indeed the opposition that arose to the library included groups that would have been divided on ethnic, economic, and ideological lines. But when the issue was posed as that of the community versus city hall and the big interests, the task of uniting the neighborhood was made far easier. It is also very likely that there was no single Ocean Hill-Brownsville position on education prior to the development of crisis-level conflicts in those neighborhoods. In fact, we would expect these neighborhoods to contain a multiplicity of different individual, block, and ethnic complaints about education. But when the issue became that of Ocean Hill-Brownsville versus the city —and when symbolic issues of institutional racism and colonialism were articulated—the task of mobilizing these neighborhoods as a coherent body was made easier. In this sense the use of symbolic issues is a simple tactic in the process of mobilizing a neighborhood and of creating a neighborhood interest out of many diverse interests. The black neighborhoods, through their symbolic conflicts, became political communities containing political resources and a sense of solidarity that they had not possessed before.

Fifth, because of the number of different groups involved in the city's street-fighting pluralism—each of which believes it has a valid interest in the decision—the resort to symbolic issues has the important function of elevating a particular group, at least in its own eyes, above mere interest group politics. Seen in these terms the Greenwich Village residents were not merely registering an aesthetic perference about the development of Washington Square that differed from the preference of New York University. By making this dispute a matter of institutions versus the neighborhood, they were able to avoid and/or transcend straightforward conflicts of interests. Further, they reduced the ambiguity of the issues and their vulnerability to counterargument by climbing on to the higher plane of symbolic issues. Had they not reached for broader symbolic issues, the fact that the neighborhood's specific objections to the library were often groundless might have seriously hurt the neighborhood position in both mobilizing support at home and dealing with city hall. Turned into a symbolic issue and a crusade to defend the neighborhood, however, the Greenwich Village group did not have to argue the case point by point. They merely had to appeal for the support of the preservation of their neighborhood—a position that is far more difficult to oppose than local objections to buildings of a certain size and scale.

Whatever legitimacy may have existed in the rough-hewn division of power between the board of education and the Ocean Hill-Brownsville community board was dissolved, at least from the community point of view, when the issue was cast in broader terms of racism and community control. Having reached for these symbols, the community no longer had to worry about or fight about the technicalities of transferring teachers. Once dramatic symbolic issues had been articulated, there was justification for bold action against the board of education. And then who could care much about the mere technicalities of administrative procedure that in the beginning lay at the heart of the dispute?

More generally my proposition is that symbolic issues will increase as the number of participants increases and the game of street-fighting pluralism becomes more unmanageable for any single player. This occurs because the ability of any player to contain the conflict and control the decision process diminishes as the number of players increases. To this extent urban players, including the mayor, will find (or fear) that their conventional political resources, such as formal governmental powers and administrative expertise, will provide inadequate bargaining strength in many-sided decision games. If this is so, major institutional players will come to resemble community groups, who turn to symbolic issues because they fear that their political resources put them at a clear disadvantage as compared to the resources of other players. My first proposition, then, is that as the number of participants increases, the ability of any player to contain and control the decision process decreases. Each player will feel increasingly powerless and will seek symbolic issues as a way of increasing political strength. Note that there is a crucial difference between the case where community groups use symbolic issues to fight entrenched institutional interests and the case where major institutions use symbolic issues in fragmented, multisided games. The difference is that in the first case one player, for example, the board of education, may indeed have disproportionate political resources vis-à-vis another, for example, a small neighborhood group. In the second case no single player is likely to have disproportionate power, and each player is likely to feel relatively powerless in the face of the combined power of all the other different players. From the perspective of any particular player it is impossible to win the game easily because so much power is held by the other contestants even though the other players are divided and fighting with one another.

In the New York City cases the players increasingly turned to symbolic issues to improve their political position as the decision game became increasingly chaotic. This tactic, which was employed by the mayor, the unions, and the community in the transit and school strikes, involved a turning away from bargaining and negotiation and a launching of symbolic crusades against their adversaries. Thus Mayor Lindsay declared war against the power brokers in the transit strike and presented his struggle as a fight for the integrity and survival of the city. The central point is that in the extreme cases of street-fighting pluralism considered here, any player will be strongly motivated to employ dramatic, polarizing, symbolic issues. Highly symbolic issues and political crusades were also launched by the teachers' union in the school strike and by the various community groups and school decentralization conflicts. Albert Shanker presented his union's position as a crusade against black anti-Semitism and in favor of due process and the fundamental rights of public employees. It should be obvious, too, that the neighborhood group in the school decentralization conflicts built its political position almost entirely on the strength of symbolic issues: racism, power to the people, and oppression of the ordinary citizen by the bureaucratic system.

If symbolic issues are used in the extreme cases of street-fighting pluralism as a defensive response to a sense of relative powerlessness, there are also more positive, political, and pragmatic reasons why symbolic issues are employed and why symbolic issues are useful to the players. First, the mayor and other players will often use symbolic issues as a way of building coalitions in a multisided decision game. Because symbolic issues tend to polarize, a mayor can seek to gain allies in a decision by enunciating a sharp them-versus-us dichotomy or by appealing to symbolic values that other players are thought to share intensely. Lindsay attempted to rally support to his position in the transit strike by attacking the power brokers and by implication defending city government and its citizens against blackmail. Other players can play the same game with symbolic issues. Shanker used the symbolic issues of black racism and public employees' rights to rally support in city bureaucracies, and particularly in the board of education, against the community.

The second positive function of polarizing symbolic issues follows directly from the first. Symbolic issues can be used by the urban players to gain support from the broader audience of urban policy making—in particular, the media, the public at large, and higher-level government. Appeals to this broad audience can have two quite different purposes. It can involve the attempt to mobilize support directly as when a mayor who takes a stand against a union or a governor is made into a martyr by the press. Or it can reduce criticism and pressure from the urban audience by explaining and justifying one's position in noble, symbolic terms.

Consider the mayor. More than the other players he is highly sensitive to the reactions of his audiences in the media, the public, and higher-level governments because he is the visible decision maker who is apt to be blamed directly for the fact that the garbage has not been picked up or the schools reopened. In terms of recent events Mayor Abraham Beame is pictured as failing to solve New York City's fiscal crisis, and the symbolism of the crisis is of

Beame fighting with the governor, the banks, and the federal government over the future and control of city government and its finances. Since urban problems are portrayed as the mayor's particular personal prolems, and urban decisions are personalized in a way that makes the mayor appear to be the main actor, it is only natural for the mayor to pay careful attention to his reputation with his audiences.

There are two sorts of issues involved here. First, the public and higher-level governments may intervene directly to support or put pressure on the mayor. The local newspaper may editorialize for or against his position. The public may rally to his stand or, in the case of a strike, place heavy pressure on city hall to solve the problem even if it will cost additional city money. Finally state or national officials may endorse the mayor by praising his strong stand, or undermine him by wondering out loud whether he has lost control of his city, or by sending intermediaries to help him (an act that implies that he is incapable of governing on his own without higher-level help).

It is certainly true that the costs and benefits to the mayor of support or opposition in his audience are hard to measure precisely, but given the difficulty the mayor has in mobilizing support in the most difficult cases of street-fighting pluralism, it stands to reason that any additional support is distinctly helpful and any additional opposition from the mayor's audience only makes matters worse.

Second, the mayor is naturally worried about his reputation in a broader sense. He has to be; after the decisions are made and conflicts are resolved, the mayor will have made some enduring impression of competence or incompetence, of ability or inability to govern his city. By his actions he will have further shaped his own reputation with his broad, urban audience. The political perils in the matter of reputation are clear: Lindsay became the mayor who could not handle the unions and Beame became the professional accountant and comptroller who could not balance his own books.

Because of the likelihood of having his reputation eroded in the most fragmented decision games, the mayor will be motivated to use symbolic issues to put his performance in the best possible light for his larger audience. Thus if the sanitation strike could be defined as a valiant struggle against power brokers, the media might not criticize the mayor so sharply for his failure to resolve the strike rapidly. Or if the mayor could be seen in the sanitation strike to be defending the city against callous takeover attempts by the state government, attention might be diverted from the daily hardships of the strike, and blame might be shifted away from the mayor's failure to end the strike. To this extent symbolic appeals to the media and public audiences were not merely good public relations; they were essential to the mayor's defense of a fundamental but very fragile political resource: the reputation for being competently, if not creatively, able to govern the city.

A corollary proposition is that a loss in reputation for being able to govern competently is not limited to the particular decision that damaged the reputation in the first place. Rather the loss of reputation in one decision game carries over to the other games and contributes to the erosion of the mayor's political authority. Another corollary is that the reputation for executive competence is easier to lose than to increase; because of the difficulty of solving urban problems, failures are both more likely and more visible and easier to measure than successes. If these arguments are at all persuasive, it becimes clear why a mayor clearly has reason to use symbolic appeals to his audience in difficult, multisided decision games.

In an article written in 1969 James Q. Wilson took what he called the "new breed" of progressive mayors to task for playing to their liberal audience in the media, foundations, and federal agencies by adopting liberal postures and policies at the same time that they ignored the more conservative feelings of their largely white constituencies. Wilson offered the following examples of this perceived pattern:

Whenever a clear choice confronts a mayor, he tends (again, especially in the big cities) to side with the liberal (though rarely the radical) side even when the liberal side appears to be widely unpopular. John Lindsay favored a civilian review board for the police, though any sounding of opinion would have shown that the vast majority of New York voters were strongly opposed to the board. Joseph Alioto became, as mayor, a backer of the police-community relations unit of the San Francisco police department even though the unit was detested by many civilians for allegedly "siding with the criminals" against the police. The response of Jerome Cavanagh to the fearful riot in Detroit was to appoint and actively support a "New Detroit Committee" that consulted with (though did not satisfy) the most militant blacks and urged programs and patience rather than tanks and toughness. And he did this though he was facing an organized campaign among white voters to recall him from office for alleged failures to curb rising crime.[15]

Wilson may well be accurate in detecting a liberal bias in the mayors he talks about, but in terms of analysis he misses a crucial point: how to maintain a reputation in the face of difficult decisive problems. Mayors have strong incentives to raise the kinds of symbolic issues that will gain them support, confidence, and goodwill in the media. Given the conventional wisdom of the 1960s that any competent mayor should take a strongly activist role in searching for policies that might alleviate urban and/or racial problems, it is entirely understandable that these mayors should have publicly espoused the policies that Wilson describes. Whether these policies were sound or misguided is a separate question. I am talking about the politics of "position taking" and more precisely about a mayor's use of symbolic issues to gain or preserve support among media audiences who, on a day-to-day basis, serve as power arbiters of the mayor's reputation for competence and intiative.[16] Symbolic politics of this sort were indeed very costly, but saying that now does not deny the appeal of symbolic issues then.

Symbolic issues have a third important positive function in urban decision making: they provide a way for different players to define the problem in terms that are most advantageous to them. Because of the subjectivity and diversity of street-level perceptions of urban problems, it is often difficult to define the nature of any particular policy problem. Different participants tend to define the problem in different ways, as they did, for example, in the hospital site controversy discussed earlier. The instability and tenuousness of problem definition in urban policy making thus leads different players to fight over the definition of the problem. In doing so, they may be able to confine or expand the boundaries of the problem, make it a crisis or a routine issue, and, most important, set the agenda of substantive questions that must be contested in the decision. The greater the number of players in a game, the greater the contest will be over the definition of the problem and the greater the value of symbolic issues. The reason is straightforward. Because symbolic issues are dramatic and polarizing they serve to define the problem in a sharp and powerful way.

Consider the utility of symbolic issues again from the perspective of the mayor. In the transit strike, the mayor could have presented his case against the city in terms of the need to keep costs and salaries down and ensure orderly processes of collective bargaining. There is not much dramatic appeal in that. But if the issue is defined as a crusade against power brokers and blackmailers, the mayor's decision to take a stubborn stand against wage increases gains justification.

Symbolic issues can be used equally well in this way by unions and community groups. If the New York University-Greenwich Village conflict had been defined as one of architectural design or park use, there might have been little potential for controversy and alliance building. But if the problem becomes one of "racism" or the "rape" of the neighborhood, the particular complaints take on a far greater meaning. The terms of the conflict are substantially changed. Obviously, it is one thing to support a famous architect's library design against people who do not like it; it is quite another to defend New York University's attempt to destroy the park and take over the neighborhood.

The trouble is that although symbolic issues have considerable political utility, they also extract heavy costs for urban government. When street-fighting pluralism encompasses a number of contradictory crusades, each supported by powerful political symbols, the prospects for containing or resolving the political conflict are generally reduced. And to the extent that urban players are drawn to highly symbolic issues (and the more participants, the more they adopt fighting symbols), each player improves his political resources in the short run but makes the city increasingly difficult, if not impossible, to govern in the long run.

Urban Decision Games and Game Playing: A Reappraisal

An analysis of the difficulty of governing the city in the face of decision games characterized by large numbers of participants (many of whom are independent of city hall) and by the introduction of highly charged, symbolic issues is sharply at variance with the most influential existing account of urban decision making and game playing: Norton Long's "The Local Community as an Ecology of Games"[17] stresses the number and diversity of urban games and presents two main arguments. First, there is a well-worked-out ecology of games; urban policy making is divided into a considerable number of small and relatively stable games, each with its own players, rules, and territory. According to Long, "In the territorial system there is a political game, a banking game, a contracting game, a newspaper game, a civic organization game and many others. Within each game, there is a well-established set of goals whose achievement indicates success or failure for the participants, a set of socialized roles making participants' behavior highly predictable, a set of strategies and tactics handed down through experience and occasionally subject to improvement and change. . . . Within the game the players can be rational in the varying degrees that the structure permits. At the very least, they know how to behave, and they know the score." He adds, "Individuals may play in a number of games, but, for the most part, their preoccupation is with one, and their sense of major achievement is through success in one."[18]

Long's second major assertion is that the ecology of games and the game playing that defines it work fairly well: "The ecology of games in the local territorial system accomplishes unplanned but largely functional results. The games and their players match in their particular pursuits to bring about the overall results; the territorial system is fed and ordered; its inhabitants are rational within limited areas and pursuing the ends of these areas, accomplish socially functional ends."[19]

I certainly do not dispute Long's contention that urban policy making consists of a large number of different decision games. Nor do I dispute that in each game there is a quality of ritual and dramatic play acting. Where my analysis does depart from Long's is in the appraisal of the character and consequences of the so-called ecology of games. First, in contrast to Long, I argue that urban games are highly unstable because different players, issues, and problems combine in an unpredictable way to produce a barrage of demands that urban policy makers must constantly react to. Second, I suggest that the players in urban decisions do not follow established, stable rules and rituals. Rather as the number of players increases (as they so often do), urban decision games turn into unstructured, unstable free-for-alls (street-fighting pluralism). Third, and more important, urban games and game playing often do not produce largely functional results, as Long asserts, "such that the territorial system is fed and ordered." Quite the contrary; decision games lead to spasms of activity, stalemates, and blind, evolutionary searches for some kind of solution to pressing problems. Moreover in urban games like those in New York City, the decision-making process had a destructive, zero-sum character. The territorial system was not being fed or ordered; it was being torn apart. Put another way the ecology of games was not in equilibrium such that unplanned actions by different players in different territories produced harmonious results. Rather the games produced street fights that left most (if not all) players feeling bitter and defeated. Fourth, whereas Long sees rational calculation and behavior in urban games, I suggest that as street-fighting pluralism increases, the games become more emotional, reactive, and irrational. This was evident in the New York City cases where the conflicts escalated to the point where they became shouting matches and crusades against evil.

Mario Cuomo, who served as mediator of the Forest Hills dispute over a low-income housing complex, has written about the character and consequences of urban game playing. He notes early in his diary, without any apparent criticism intended, that urban decision making is a "game." But by the end he is speaking of fraud, shamming, "doing a number," and "sand bagging." In this view urban game playing becomes destructive and even ugly. Cuomo says, "Dozens of misconceptions have been generated and are frequently believed and brandished by people in this controversy. It is difficult to tell whether this is the result of intellectual slippage, the efficacy of demagoguery, or a simple fabrication by the people involved. But, if they are fabrications, then I've met some of the best actors in New York City outside of the Broadway stage." There can be no denying the emotion and ugliness of the

conflict in which the opponents to public housing wind up scream-
ing at a public hearing: "My wife will be mugged and raped and
you ask me to be reasonable."[20] In short Long's relatively placid,
stable ecology of games simply does not provide an adequate account of the conflicts engendered by street-fighting pluralism in
what has become an increasingly ungovernable city.

6
Mayors and Their Political Strategies

The mayor stands at the center of the city's reactive, unstable policy-making system. Because of the extreme fragmentation of political institutions and citizen demands within them, big-city mayors daily confront the entrenched power of many feudal barons in the scores of boards, commissions, professional service bureaucracies, and state and federal agencies that surround him and constrain his leadership. He is a highly visible and vulnerable target of a great number of different street-level demands coming from individuals, blocks, community organizations, unions, ethnic groups, and countless other interest groups. Every day he and his administration deliver (or fail to deliver) basic services to millions of urban residents, and these citizens, however organized and represented, have no reluctance at all to fight city hall to get more of what they want in whatever way they can. In the face of these very different decision games, the mayors of large U.S. cities, faced with the unenviable task of making an increasingly ungovernable city governable, must adopt various leadership styles and political strategies.

Mayors differ along two central dimensions: (1) the amount of political and financial resources that they possess in dealing with their various problems and (2) the degree of activism and innovation that they display in their daily work. The two dimensions permit the identification of four ideal types that correspond closely to the mayoral styles in the largest cities. We will not attempt to define in detail the different leadership styles at the outset, but will introduce them briefly and then show how the styles are manifest in the behavior of a number of America's better-known mayors.

One style is that of the mayor who possesses weak political and financial resources but who exhibits a strong desire to solve urban problems and produce significant policy innovations. I will call this the crusader style. The crusader emphasizes a symbolic politics and crisis management because he does not have the resources to govern and control the city consistently through the force of political or financial clout. Instead, he must dramatize issues and develop support through the force of his principles and personality. The Lindsay administration in New York illustrated this approach to urban problem solving.[1]

A second style tends toward the mayor who possesses strong political and/or fiscal resources and who also takes a strongly activist posture toward urban policy making. This is the style of the entrepreneur. The entrepreneur uses his available political and fiscal resources to provide large-scale public projects and other new public services to build and consolidate political support. Richard C. Lee of New Haven is an illustration of this type.[2]

A third style is that of the mayor who possesses strong political and/or fiscal resources but who assumes a passive attitude toward urban problem solving. This is the style of the boss. The boss uses his political resources to maintain political control. His motto could be "Don't Make No Waves; Don't Back No Losers."[3] Richard Daley of Chicago was a classic example.[4]

The final style of political leadership is that of the mayor who possesses relatively weak political and/or fiscal resources and who also assumes a passive role in urban policy making. It is the style of the broker. The broker accepts the limitations of his power and seeks to keep peace in the city by carefully balancing and adjusting conflicts, demands, and interests. Robert Wagner and Abraham Beame of New York are illustrations of this type.[5]

The political strategies adopted by crusaders, entrepreneurs, bosses, and brokers are best demonstrated by their characteristic behavior and policy responses.

The Mayor as Crusader

More than a decade has passed since John Lindsay first ran for mayor, pledging to make "New York the Empire City once again." His administration would show, he promised, that large cities were still governable. According to his campaign posters, he was fresh and everyone else was tired.[7] Now John Lindsay is tired too, and his ebullient promise to master and reform New York government has been replaced by self-deprecatory jokes about the virtue of mere survival in the urban jungle. As it turned out John Lindsay was succeeded in office by the man he defeated in 1965. In the highly cyclical world of urban politics, it is perhaps not too surprising or ironic that Abe Beame campaigned successfully on the pledge that he could put the pieces together again and make the ungovernable city governable.

Viewed from the perspective of the mid-1970s, Lindsay takes on lasting significance as a big city mayor because he is a distinctive product of the urban-crisis era of the 1960s. He is a particularly interesting example of this era in urban politics because he took office after the first entrepreneurial successes of urban renewal had been achieved, and he stayed on to face the whirlwind produced by black protest, community control, blue-collar protest, militant public unionism, welfare problems, and declining federal commitment to the cities. Lindsay was thus at first the product of a buoyant public mood that supported political intervention, experimentation, and risk taking, but in his last years he was forced to respond to a public mood that viewed urban crusaders with suspicion and resentment and city life itself with increasing frustration and fear.

Setting the Lindsay administration in this political context, it is easy to see why Lindsay, like so many other mayors, suffered a steady erosion of popularity within the city and reputation outside of it. Had he been able to manipulate his own political personality so that he could, by turns, present himself as a crusading reformer, a tough cop, a budget cutter, a power broker, and a skilled labor negotiator, he might now be serving a third term. However most politicians are only once-born—and at most twice-born—and the recent emergence of Lindsay, the management efficiency specialist, can hardly disguise his original and enduring incarnation as Lindsay the Reformer. Lindsay was hired to solve the city's fundamental problems, not to improve the maintenance and repair of sanitation trucks. It is Lindsay as a crusading reformer who deserves careful assessment and whose successes and failures carry an important message not only about the reform tradition but about the future of city politics.

Symbolic Politics

Like all other political regimes, the Lindsay administration expressed a fascinating blend of policy and political personality. Lindsay's basic political style was to dramatize urban problems

through moralistic rhetoric and force of personality. It is worth re-
membering that this political style fulfilled the expectations held
by many people in 1965 about what dynamic political leadership
should be. Nevertheless it was a distinctive political style and strategy with a clear logic and, as it turned out, with clear benefits and
costs.

One consequence of this personalized and highly dramatized
politics was that Lindsay had to spend a great deal of his time out on
the streets "showing the flag." And it is hard, to say the least, to
control the machinery of government and be in a position to react
thoughtfully to new events and crises while moving from one public engagement or trouble spot to another in the official limousine.
For this reason the political style of crusaders like Lindsay tends to
be frantic and breathless: they are perpetually caught in the process of rushing to the next fire.

More important the political leader who seeks to dramatize reform must inevitably rely heavily on symbolic politics. Like most
other activist mayors of the late 1960s, Lindsay lacked the fiscal
resources to solve the economic aspects of the urban crisis immediately. And no less than any other American citizen, he lacked a
clear understanding of what it would mean and what it would take
to solve all the other aspects of urban problems. What Lindsay
could do was express concern and commitment. He could dramatize the problems of the urban poor by being seen in their midst
and by visiting their houses, their schools, and their playgrounds.
When riots threatened New York and other cities, he went to the
angry neighborhoods and gave a human and empathetic expression to the idea of city hall. He could cool the streets, and he did. It
is hard to imagine that a mayor lacking Lindsay's ability to dramatize and symbolize in his public presence could have been as effective.

At that moment Lindsay received high praise, for it was unques-
tionably in the public interest of every New Yorker to prevent rioting and bloodshed in the city. In this one case the symbolism of
concern worked well. It was not only excellent political theater, it
was excellent politics as well. However, even at the time of his
greatest triumph, Lindsay's symbolic politics had their cost. A
strong commitment to a principle or a constituency implies (if the

initial commitment is serious) that competing principles and constituencies cannot be embraced with equal fervor. In the rough
logic of the political arena, to be problack meant to be indifferent
or hostile to the white working class. Of course, as long as the
threat of riots made this apparent prejudice a civic virtue, Lindsay
could have it both ways. But unhappily for the mayor and his symbolic politics, issues and public attention change overnight in the
turbulent world of urban politics. With all the diversity of need and
interest in the city, it is almost impossible for one issue and one
citizen interest to hold center stage for long. And in any case urban
residents have short memories when it comes to services rendered
by political leaders. As Warren Moscow aptly puts it, "What have
you done for me lately?"[8] is the eternal question in city politics. In
Lindsay's case, the strategy employed to deal with fires in Harlem
was of no use in handling snow removal in Queens. The political
symbolism that allowed him to succeed so well in the one case
became a damaging handicap in the other. For this reason symbolic politics are a crude instrument, poorly suited to building viable
political coalitions. The tendency in dramatizing issues is to dichot-
omize the world into good guys and villains by posing conflicts
more sharply and unambiguously than they deserve. This tendency was particularly vivid in Lindsay's handling of the early public
union strikes. When the transit strike began on the same day he
took office, he immediately reached for the sharp, dichotomizing
symbols that were to serve him so well in dealing with ghetto un-
rest. The city was being exploited by the "power brokers," he said,
and his administration would not do business with blackmailers. In
climbing on to this lofty rhetorical perch, Lindsay successfully dramatized the union conflict as a straight fight between the public
interest (which he represented) and selfish greed (represented by
the unnamed power brokers). In this case symbolic politics made
good theater but poor politics. The embattled mayor may have
appeared as a courageous martyr, but the public suffered the consequences. Lindsay made his point, but so did Mike Quill (vivid
political symbolism can be used by players on both sides), and a
settlement was finally reached after a long strike and at a price in
wages that made a mockery of the mayor's resolve.

The costs of symbolic politics were even more obvious in the ensuing sanitation strike. Lindsay again reached for the symbols of public integrity versus private greed, depicting himself as the martyred victim of another gang of bandits and power brokers. This time, according to the polls, Lindsay did gain public favor for his courage, but the costs of moralism were great. The public suffered along with its mayor, and this must surely have reduced the political value of moralism. People admire the martyr quality in public leaders as long as they can admire the commitment to principle form afar and not be forced to pay the costs of its expression. Nelson Rockefeller was cast in the role of the back-room fixer in the sanitation strike, and he lost popularity in the polls. He also helped settle the strike and saved the mayor from an intractable problem. What is most revealing is that Lindsay's dramatizing, symbolizing style gradually eroded during his term in office. Having worked well in cooling the streets, it could not be sustained in dealing with issues involving tangled, multisided conflicts in which many different power games, vested interests, and political symbols came into collision. By the end of his first term, Lindsay apparently had recognized the persistence of old-style politics and was using the tools of patronage, back-room bargaining (with labor unions), and patient compromise (with opposed interest groups) with considerable relish.[9] Of course by 1970 he was also living in a different political world. The mayor whose assistants helped write a strong condemnation of white racism into the Kerner Commission report was laboring hard to fix potholes in Brooklyn and improve service delivery in middle-income Jewish neighborhoods.

If the reform style of the dramatizing crusader has shown itself to be effective under the special conditions presented by urban rioting but highly costly in others, what can be said of other leadership styles that might be employed by mayors in the urban world of the mid- and late 1970s? In the first place, it appears that two classic urban leadership styles and strategies are unlikely to predominate in the short run in the large cities. The first style is that of the political entrepreneur. In the hands of a Lee of New Haven or a Richardson Dilworth of Philadelphia, the entrepreneurial style was a powerful and, in Lee's case, an overpowering political weapon.[10] Lee provided new department stores, highways, and parking garages for the central business district, thus giving tangible economic benefits to numerous producers and consumers. He rehabilitated one neighborhood, built a commercial and service center in another, and located moderate-income housing and housing for the elderly throughout the city. It is a measure of the success of Lee's strategy that serious opposition to him developed only at the end of his sixteen-year regime—and then at the height of rioting and protest taking place in all American cities.

The political logic of the entrepreneurial style is that support can be gained through projects and programs that confer new benefits on particular groups of citizens. In this strategy one success produces the political capital that permits a new investment that further extends benefits and widens support. However, without large-scale public projects, it is quite clear that the entrepreneurial style will be difficult to reproduce in the 1970s. The federal money is not there, and the public appetite for and patience with large-scale physical and social engineering has plainly been reduced. Abe Beame, Tom Bradley (Los Angeles), and Kevin White (Boston) simply lack the political and fiscal resources to build a dynasty on their performance as master builders.

Modern mayors of today typically have lacked sufficiently broad support in their communities to play the classical role of political bosses. The growth of nonwhite populations and the development of new political tensions between different white ethnic groups and neighborhoods make it very difficult to run the kind of old-fashioned political machine based on a dominant working-class base and ethnic solidarity. In Chicago and, to a greater extent, in cities like Albany, the classical machine has hung on, but this has been a triumph of persistence, not of invention. In addition it is hard to see alternative machine coalitions in the making. The prospects for growth of new black machines have been undermined by conflict and apathy in poor communities, the reduction of patronage (given civil service and the end of the war on poverty), and by the need of the new black mayors to seek accommodations with powerful white interests.

Given the fragmentation of urban politics, the most likely leadership style to emerge is that of the cautious political broker, carefully balancing and compromising different political interests. This style, with its emphasis on balancing ethnic interests and avoiding sharp political and symbolic conflicts, is indeed the style that mayors like Beame, Bradley, and even Richard Hatcher of Gary, Indiana, seem naturally to favor.[11] The strength of this style, as practiced consummately by Robert Wagner in the 1950s, is its stolid but steady adjustment of sharply divergent interests and thus its ability to maintain a broad but uneasy coalition. The appearance of political control and harmony is furthered by the cautious political broker, even if many important issues and problems are avoided, evaded, or negotiated away. On the other hand the weakness of the style clearly lies in its lack of imagination, innovation, and risk taking. Under the cautious broker, street-fighting pluralism will rarely erupt into civil war, but the city's fundamental problems are likely to receive only a halting, piecemeal treatment.

Strategies of Management

As a reformer and the candidate of the minority Republican party, John Lindsay entered city hall with limited political resources. There was no machine behind him and no sweeping electoral mandate either. Even more important he had reason to wonder whether he was even the master in his own house, the vast city bureaucracy. Some of the city's bureaucracies, like police and fire, were distinctly independent and were run in the old-fashioned manner as Irish fiefdoms. Sanitation was Italian, and various other departments were heavily staffed by political appointees from the Wagner era. From Lindsay's perspective the parts of the bureaucracy that were not controlled by hostile Irish and Italian clubs or by political hacks were likely to be dominated by old-line bureaucrats—another scourge of liberal reformers. Faced with this kind of bureaucracy (or, at least, perceiving this kind of bureaucracy), Lindsay (and many other reformers) centralized power in the hands of a few mayoral aides, attempted to introduce strong administrative control through scientific management, and, in general, tried to shake up the outmoded, recalcitrant bureaucracy through guerrilla raids from city hall. Lindsay's bid for administrative control of his government was made through the deployment of "whiz kid" assistants, highly professional budgeters, and scientific managers such as the McKinsey Corporation and the New York City Rand Institute. The record of his aides and technocrats was occasionally brillant, occasionally disastrous, more often erratic, and almost always revealing.

In building his first administration around young assistants like Jay Kriegel, Sid Davidoff, and Barry Gottehrer, Lindsay gained the dedication and energy he needed to weather the crisis politics of his first years. He also gained the zeal and self-confidence he needed in his attempt to shake up and control the city bureaucracy. At the same time his strategy gave to his administration a set of pronounced ideological preconceptions (if not blinders). Even more than their mayor the Lindsay assistants believed that the bureaucracy was full of incompetents and that their role was to beat it into shape through the use of superior intelligence and industry—and if that failed, through whatever political muscle could be found lying around city hall. Equally important, the mayor's aides, some of whom had been involved in the civil-rights movement, had a very clear idea of who the good guys and villains were in city politics. Finally, the aides reinforced the mayor's almost chiliastic view of urban leadership. They believed that the city was dangerously close to complete collapse, and their job was to save it.

Like their mayor the young aides had genuine triumphs in working at the street level to cool racial tension, but their efforts to deal with bureaucracies, unions, and, in particular, the school strike led to costly political failure and embarrassing fiascos. In particular, their assaults on bureaucracies like the police department were not only ineffectual but also produced deep alienation in the bureaucracy. In the Ocean Hill-Brownsville crises, their ideological attachment to the poor and disdain for the white middle class (and their representatives) paved the way to the bitter polarization that ensued.

Lindsay's strategy of running the city with a small group of city hall shock troops exhibited all the familiar problems of highly centralized and personalized administration.

For all their energy the city hall aides were unable to control the city from the top. It proved difficult, if not impossible, to improve coordination and communication in city government when most important political communications were routed by design through the city hall switchboard. It has often been remarked that decision making in the Lindsay administration suffered from a political and administrative overload at the center—an overload that led to frantic activity and crisis management.[12] It is important to realize that these administrative pressures were created by the decision-making structure itself, as well as by the crush of external demands.

If the city hall aides were continually thwarted in their attempt to tie together the intricate lines of power and control in the city, commissioners and high-ranking civil servants were also frustrated and sometimes bitter about their relationship with city hall. With policy making centralized in the mayor's office, the commissioners and other top administrators were relatively isolated. They rarely saw the mayor and dealt instead with the aides assigned to oversee their departments. Some commissioners bitterly resented what they perceived to be the interference and arrogance of the mayor's young aides. Others took advantage of their isolation and built up independent baronies in areas of policy making that city hall was not riding herd on. Either way the result was to create a significant gap between top-level policy making and day-to-day administration that impeded both policy coordination and program implementation. At lower levels of the bureaucracy among rank-and-file civil servants, Lindsay's administrative strategy caused even harder feelings. Civil servants often felt that they were held in contempt by the young mayoral assistants and that no one in city hall was interested in their expertise and ideas. Some, especially the veterans, could not tolerate the thought that they were being ordered around by young people with little experience in New York or in city government. Thus the strategy of shaking up the bureaucracy from the top encountered not only the expected bureaucratic inertia and rigidity but, more important, deep-seated personal hostility toward the movers and shakers on the part of the "shook."

Entrepreneurs like Richard Lee avoid the crusader's staffing and management problems by building their own administrative apparatus.[13] Lee did this by using urban renewal and antipoverty funds to develop bureaucratic instruments that amounted to a private governmental structure. Thus the New Haven Redevelopment

Agency and Community Progress gave him the ability to bypass completely old-line bureaucracies in designing and implementing new programs. Once he creates new institutions to work through, the entrepreneurial mayor has no need to depend on the problematic talents of aides and scientific managers. Rather he has the ability to recruit strong, independent managers and give them the authority and the resources to run their own operations. This is what Lee was able to do with Edward Logue in urban renewal and with Mitchell Sviridoff in the poverty program. This too was the strategy of Richardson Dilworth and Joseph Clark in Philadelphia; and it is interesting that Robert Moses gained his prominence and power as an urban planner and administrator working through new institutions created, in part, by the La Guardia administration.[14] Of course the entrepreneur's strategy of building new institutions to run the city works best (and perhaps only) when substantial new resources exist, for the task of reforming and redirecting existing bureaucracies is more difficult by far than building new ones according to the mayor's personal specifications. In this context it is worth noting that the Lindsay administration achieved its greatest administrative initiative and control in areas of the government where it was able to develop new bureaucratic instruments: the Project Management staff, the Office of Neighborhood Government, and certain newly developed areas of the Housing and Human Resources Administration.

Of all mayors the boss, with his dominant political resources, has the simplest approach to staffing and administration. His administrative stretegy reflects his need to maintain the strength of his political machine, and the strength of his machine gives coherence and loyalty to his administration. The boss fills his administration with party workers, and he has strong control over their work because he can replace them at will. In turn he has a strong incentive to stay in close touch with and be responsive to his bureaucrats because his political strength depends on having large numbers of satisfied loyal party workers. In the boss case in general, and in the case of Richard Daley's Chicago in particular, the political and administrative systems of the city become mutually reinforcing—indeed become a seamless web.

The broker's staffing and management problem is more subtle than that of the boss or entrepreneur but clearly less frustrating than that of the crusading reformer. Lacking the political resources to build new institutions or to erect a comprehensive patronage/ exchange system, the broker must use his appointment powers to construct and maintain political coalitions. He must be responsive to the job claims of groups that can exercise power at the bargaining table. And, finally, he must carefully cultivate and reward the constituency that he is most dependent on in running the city: the civil service bureaucracy that can support or frustrate him in many different ways every day. In New York City the broker's style was vividly exhibited in the Wagner administration, and it appears that it is now being fully restored by Abe Beame. In Wagner's hands the broker strategy meant a careful representation of different ethnic groups, the elevation of veteran city bureaucrats, and the establishment of close political relationships with public union leaders. The last relationship became so cozy that at least one writer, Theodore Lowi, has suggested that Wagner was trying to build a new machine on the strength of civil service support.[15] However, this view forgets that Wagner's key partners in city hall were "old pro" politicians and bureaucrats and that, for all of his cultivation of union leaders, their relationship remained at root an adversary one subject to constant bargaining and renegotiation. In short Wagner was not trying to build a new machine, he was merely trying to keep his fences mended and to maintain a delicate omnibus coalition of reformers, white ethnics, minority group leaders, organization Democrats, career bureaucrats, and union leaders.

Abe Beame's staffing and management strategy bears a remarkable resemblance to Wagner's. As an aspiring broker, Beame seems to have adopted wholesale the administrative techniques of his Democratic predecessor. Like Wagner, Beame has constructed the administrative version of a balanced ticket in city hall. Although some minority group leaders have been dissatisfied by their share of top-level administrative patronage, it is clear that the mayor has followed an explicit strategy of group representation. Also like Wagner, Beame has appointed enough party regulars to keep his county political leaders content, though he has by no means filled up city hall with clubhouse politicians. Even more than Wagner, Beame has built his administration on an alliance with the professional civil service. Rather than attacking old-line bureaucrats, as Lindsay did, or bypassing them, as Lee did in New Haven, Beame has made them his senior partners in government. The problem of the Beame administration is thus not whether the mayor can communicate with and control his bureaucracy; rather it is whether the professional civil service, now that it has gained power and authority, can also muster the energy, imagination, and flexibility to put together the pieces of urban government.

Dilemmas of Innovation

In trying to make New York the Empire City once again, John Lindsay not only sought to reform existing structures; he also wished to innovate on a broad scale and thus turn a sluggish government into an adventurous one—constantly testing new programs and solving problems in new ways. This, of course, is the reformer's time-honored conception of what an aggressive, activist government should do. In practice, however, the task of translating new ideas into effective programs and policies is full of difficulties and dilemmas. In particular innovation is a tricky business for a crusading mayor who wants to turn his city around in a hurry. The problem for a mayor like John Lindsay is that his political strategy cannot support the kind of careful, small-scale innovations that are most likely to work in a tangled system. The crusader is after large-scale change, not piecemeal adjustments. To make his aspirations and abilities credible, he needs to produce significant results quickly. And to generate enthusiasm and mobilize support for his leadership, he must offer highly charged ideas that capture the imagination of his constituency. It is no accident that Lyndon Johnson should design a heroic war on poverty and that John Lindsay should offer an equally ambitious program vision of decentralization, scientific management, and governmental reorganization.

Unfortunately the political logic that draws crusaders to bright, even miraculous, new innovations also leads them into a quagmire in implementation, for the only innovations that can generate widespread initial enthusiasm and support are ones that are highly

symbolic and vague and that manage to appeal to normally conflicting interests. The war on poverty appeared to offer something
to everyone in this way, and so did Lindsay's designs for decentralization.[16] In its first highly generalized form everyone liked the
idea of decentralization and neighborhood government: minority
leaders, homeowners in white neighborhoods, foundation officials, and even the leaders of the teachers' union. However, as
soon as concrete plans for decentralization were developed, there
was no longer any way to conceal the contradictory sources of initial support for the concept. Inevitably actual decentralization
experiments did not fulfill various hopes for decentralization. In
addition the crusader's desire to launch large-scale, citywide innovations added to the administrative difficulty of implementation,
and frustration quickly set in when the ambitious innovation did
not produce its promised results. Unhappily for the crusader,
when dramatic innovations like decentralization (or the war on
poverty) turn sour, they do so with a vengeance. Because they
were oversold in the first place, these innovations are rarely
judged to have been merely flawed or unlucky or to have produced
mixed results and unforeseen consequences. Rather they are
harshly repudiated, sometimes vilified. There is no idea less hon-
ored than one whose time has gone. The boom-and-bust pattern
that often afflicts dramatic innovations has two further consequences. First, disappointment with one innovation tends to sour
other innovations and the impulse toward innovation in city hall.
Thus Lindsay administrators who struggled through the decentralization battles in the schools suddenly became cautious and defensive in later plans for decentralization. They did not want to be
burned again. The second consequence is that when an innovation
is discredited by a dramatic failure, other less visible experiments
that actually work go unnoticed. This is the clear pattern with Lindsay's decentralization experiments. Innovations like community
service cabinets and some multiservice centers may well have produced significant results, but their impact was dwarfed by the
more controversial versions (and failures) of the strategy.

These dilemmas of innovation haunt the ambitious reformers far
more than mayors with different styles and strategies. The entrepreneur tends to stick to innovations in bricks and mortar that he

can deliver on. The boss has no strong impulse to innovate at all. He is trying to preserve a political and administrative system, and he devotes his energies to oiling the machinery, not creating new machinery. Finally the broker does not want to shake up fragile coalitions and bargains with jarring innovations. The trouble with the broker's leadership is that after his careful assessment of the political costs and benefits of innovation, he can usually find sufficient grounds for inaction. It is the rare innovation (of any significance) that carries with it negligible costs or even an obviously positive benefit-cost ratio.

The Federal Connection

It is increasingly obvious to big city mayors, whatever their style or strategy, that as much urban policy is made in Washington and in state capitols as in city hall. The new federalism only extends a historical trend toward growing state involvement; and the federal government, despite its apparent retreat under the new federalism, remains a crucial partner in many areas of public policy making. What this means for the mayor is that the success of his administration depends as much on his ability to deal with the federal triangle as on his ability to cope with street-fighting pluralism in his own city.

John Lindsay's strategy as a player in the federal game was, not surprisingly, highly distinctive and dramatic; it reflected his crusader style and his commitment to symbolic politics. However, more than in other aspects of his leadership, the results of the Lindsay strategy are hard to assess. Certainly Lindsay succeeded in dramatizing the crisis of the cities in his state and, to some extent, in the nation. In organizing the "big six" cities into a kind of political bloc, he provided a rallying point for urban interests in New York State. In his congressional testimony and through the media, he was a forceful advocate of urban programs and a potent symbol of its beleaguered, long-suffering chief executives. Without disputing the rhetorical force of his urban sermons, it seems clear that Lindsay's crusading style caused serious and often costly strains on the city's federal relations, for the force of Lindsay's attempt to symbolize and dramatize the city's place was to attack presidents and governors as callous enemies of the city who favored farmers and businessmen, fought wars rather than poverty, and turned their backs on the poor and nonwhite. Much has been written about the hostile relationship between John Lindsay and Nelson Rockefeller, and it is now customary to blame the feud on a clash of personalities and political ambition. There may well be some truth in these explanations, but there is an ample source of conflict in a much simpler fact: Rockefeller believed he was doing a great deal for the cities (and there is some evidence in state expenditures that he was), but Lindsay insisted on depicting him as an archfiend. The problem with Lindsay's strategy here was twofold. First, the city and the state experienced a constant level of conflict and distrust that was destructive and wasteful for both. Put another way, it is hard for a mayor to bargain effectively with higher-level governments when he is constantly making his federal partners look bad. Not only do national and state administrators lose the political credit and goodwill that work as positive incentives to further urban involvement; they also feel an incentive to retaliate against a mayor who is constantly attacking them. From the city's point of view, Lindsay's strategy of blaming higher-level government for urban problems paved the way to what might be called buck-passing federalism. Rather than gaining cooperation and coordination, the crusading mayor tends to set in motion a chain reaction of angry recriminations. The mayor blames the governor, the governor blames the president, the president blames the mayor, and many neighborhood leaders blame all three.

The process of assigning blame for urban problems to one federal partner or another might be a fruitful one if indeed the cities suffered simply from an absence of fiscal resources that higher-level governments possessed but did not choose to bestow on the cities. (Indeed, in Lindsay's more polemical statements, this is precisely the accusation.) But if urban problems are not simply resource problems but rest crucially on problems of trust, responsiveness, regulation, and restructuring, then buck-passing recriminations about fiscal stinginess and mismanagement are not only divisive but also misleading. Put simply, the Lindsay strategy had the effect both of increasing public awareness of urban problems and of antagonizing his federal counterparts, and it is the dilemma of his strategy that he probably could not have done one without the other. If this is true, John Lindsay was probably a greater asset in federal politics to the citizens of Rochester and Newark than to the citizens of New York City.

Other types of mayors seek a more cooperative and harmonious relationship with higher level governments. The entrepreneur, in the heyday of a Lee or an Allen, made a career of cultivating their federal relations and, more concretely, of working with the federal grants process to their advantage. Lee in particular built his local political power, his national reputation, and indeed his city with federal money. At root the success of entrepreneurial mayors is based on two mutually reinforcing political skills: salesmanship at home and grantsmanship abroad. By contrast the political boss typically manages his federal relations through the straightforward application of political leverage. When the mayor is a Democrat dealing with a Democratic president or governor, the federal bargain is exceptionally easy to strike. Federal programs and aid are exchanged for political support. In addition even when the mayor-boss has to deal with higher-level executives from a different party, his influence with legislators and bureaucrats in both the state and national capitols serves to maintain his political position in federalism. The boss's Achilles' heel in federal politics is corruption. If blatant corruption is being ignored by protective federal partners from the same party, a change in party control at higher levels can be fatal. Hugh Addonizio of Newark and John Kenny of Jersey City learned this fact of federal politics the hard way.

The broker's role in federal politics is a natural extension of his strategy within city government. He is careful not to make enemies and will work patiently to build up political support and make mutually beneficial bargains. He will rarely score great victories for the city in its dealings with the state and national governments, but he will also avoid damaging feuds and estrangements. Such was the record of Robert Wagner in working with New York State. He traded on the fiscal margin with Nelson Rockefeller and developed a smooth political relationship.

The Problem of Authority

Mayors of all styles and strategies face a common dilemma: gaining and maintaining political authority. Can urban leaders gain authority when they are so exposed to public demands, when they face deepening social problems, and when they typically lack the resources and the understanding to solve them? Put another way, how can they maintain their political viability when they alienate ten times as many groups as they satisfy with most decisions; when it is more likely that their solutions will fail than succeed; and when dissatisfaction with urban conditions grows in one neighborhood after another?

Viewed from this perspective, the prospects for crusading mayors like Lindsay seem especially bleak, yet at the same time their style and strategy appears most admirable. A crusader like John Lindsay was forced to risk popularity and higher office for the sake of his convictions and his commitment to help his city. Lindsay attempted to attack fundamental social problems against all odds and against any observer's better political judgment. When his dream collapsed (and even many small successes could not have sustained it), his political authority also collapsed. A weakened president can hide behind the protective shield of the Constitution and the powerful symbols of his office; a weakened mayor has no place to hide from public dissatisfaction. If Lindsay had been a United States senator, his crusading and moralizing might have earned him respect; but in city hall he had to pay the full political price for dreams that failed and administrative strategies that proved to have as many costs as benefits. In ten years it may seem clearer than it is today that no mayor could have done more than Lindsay in solving urban problems. But it is also likely to seem equally certain that many other mayors could have.

The Prospects for Mayoral Leadership

Today there are new actors in the struggle for public control: public service unions, minority group activists, leaders of defensive working-class neighborhoods, reformers, and law and order candidates. But none of these actors has the political strength to reorganize service delivery simply by force of political will. Given the social and economic diversity of urban neighborhoods, it is hard to see what kind of cohesive new political order could be established to overcome the present political fragmentation of the city. The numerical dominance of the immigrant population provided the basis for the great machines, and the dominance of white, working-class voters provided the political support in the 1950s for strong mayors like Daley and Lee. But today the political makeup of the city is increasingly fragmented; there is a mélange of low-income neighborhoods (with their own ethnic and economic divisions), defensive working-class neighborhoods, growing areas of upwardly mobile homeowners, and pockets of upper-middle-class reformism. In this context those at the top in urban government, be they active or passive, are likely to have trouble establishing effective political control over their cities. As a result entrepreneurs like Lee or Allen of Atlanta are likely to be replaced by frustrated crusaders like Lindsay. And confident bosses from Tammany Hall and men like Daley or Whalen in Jersey City are likely to be replaced by cautious political brokers. This pattern of change in leadership styles in city hall is represented in figure 3.

Figure 3. Men in city hall: leadership styles and how they might change activism/innovation

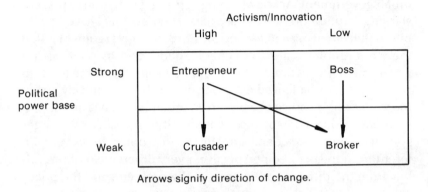

Arrows signify direction of change.

7
The Future of City Government

Urban analysts of all disciplines and dispositions are under considerable pressure today to offer miracle cures to the problems of urban government. Acknowledging a strong temptation to present startling solutions in these final pages, I confess that I have no rabbits to pull out of my hat. Indeed the burden of my argument is that the city's problems are so deeply embedded in its political and governmental structure that it would be facile, to say the least, to pretend that urban problems can be easily and quickly fixed. Moreover one's choice of a preferred urban solution is heavily dependent on one's perspective: community, city hall, or the larger system of American federalism. The urban problem looks very different from these three perspectives; very different solutions follow from the different definitions of the problem, and the policy solutions that follow from the three perspectives are in fundamental conflict with one another. In short architects of urban government are unlikely to please all the major parties to the dispute about the city problem. Nevertheless it is still a useful first step, in thinking about the future of city government, to clarify the competing perspectives, problem definitions, and policy trade-offs.

Before considering these competing perspectives as well as some proposed urban solutions I would like to underscore three structural features of the ungovernable city that must be recognized and acted upon by any workable solution. The first feature, which goes a long way toward explaining why the city is increasingly ungovernable, is that urban government is both too centralized and too decentralized. It is too centralized in the sense that even as a street-level government, the relationship between the servers and the served is not close enough to produce the responsiveness and trust on which the service relationship depends. This failing calls for greater decentralization and for a stronger partnership between citizens and public employees at the street level.

City government is also too decentralized in fundamental ways. The cost of having service bureaucracies act as relatively independent street-level governments is that there is not enough control and regulation by the center to ensure that street-level bureaucrats consistently meet qualitative and quantitative standards of performance. More important there is not enough central control to ensure that money gets spent on its intended purposes, that money is spent efficiently—at least in the sense of cost control—and that expenditures are accounted for in a way that both affirms the basic fiscal responsibilities of city government and also provides a basis for evaluating the relative effectiveness of different expenditures.

In addition because of the fragmentation among the various street-level governments, there is almost no central coordination of service programs and policies although it is clear that services provided by police, welfare, and school bureaucracies, for example, are often highly interdependent. Because of fragmentation among the service bureaucracies, the central policy makers in city hall lack an overview of the way services are packaged and allocated throughout the city, and they have almost no idea of what the city service profile is in a particular neighborhood or policy area (such as elderly services or programs to combat juvenile delinquency). Thus a mayor simply does not know what service strategy, if any, he is buying with his expenditures and how the elements of the service strategy fit together. Ask a mayor what his coverage is in services to the elderly; what service treatments are emphasized; what overlapping exists between programs; what neighborhoods are receiving disproportionately large expenditures; how many elderly residents are served by a particular program (or programs); what the comparative cost per client served is among different services for the elderly; and how high the administrative overhead is as a percentage of spending in any given program—he will be unable to answer. Even if he decided to make a study to find out what the city was doing in the area of elderly services, he might have a very difficult time finding information about how city money was being spent and with what discernible effect. This failing of urban governance and control calls for greater centralization of policy planning, coordination, and evaluation in service delivery.

There is also a second sense in which the city is too decentralized. In dealing with large-scale policy problems such as the externalities caused by population, job, and industry movements as well as problems of school financing, welfare payments, environmental protection, and urban growth, the cities are too small as governmental units to provide solutions within city limits. This is a point that has been made by generations of urban analysts, and it remains no less true today for having been repeated so often in the past. This failing of urban governance, which is not really the city's failing at all, means there should be far greater centralized planning and financing of a number of urban functions by the states and by the federal government.

The second main feature of urban governance that must be reckoned with by any workable solution is the overloaded character of the urban policy-making system. In particular the overload in the city's central nerve center at city hall makes urban policy reactive, erratic, and full of spasms and drift. In saying this, I assume that city administrators, especially the mayor, will always be primarily in the business of street-level service delivery. This is what mayors and other urban administrators have always done, what they do best, and what it is most important for them to do (given the rather different preoccupations of higher-level government). I also assume that the business of service delivery will always take place in the street fight of urban politics and will lead inevitably to some degree of instability, reactive policy making, and even crisis hopping. My hope, therefore, is not that the mayor be relieved of his historical duties or that he somehow be made into a cost-benefit analyst who surveys the urban street fight from the detached perspective of "policy analysis." Such detachment is impossible. The unavoidable feature of urban government is that its impact on urban residents is tangible, visible, and direct. The mayor is held responsible when the snow has not been cleared after a storm and when reading levels decline in the schools. If this were not the case, the importance and interest of city government as a public institution would greatly decline.

My concern is rather that city hall reduce the number of functions it must perform and to reassign some of the responsibility for managing an unmanageable number of public programs. I therefore want to make an argument for simplification, for focusing on basic urban services as a way of relieving the mayor and others in city hall from the frustration of dealing with an impossible number of demands and performing an unwieldy number of functions.

My third central concern is to reduce the burdens and costs that are placed on city government by the present system of intergovernmental policy making. The legacy of a half-century of federal and state policy has been to make city government bear even more functions, programs, and responsibilities for administrative control, regulation, and evaluation. Moreover, the city has been the cockpit of American social policy where the different levels of government try out and fight over urban problem-solving strategies. The impact of this intergovernmental contest has been to increase the overload at the center of urban policy making in city hall. The revenue-sharing strategy of the new federalism was designed in part to free the city from some of the transaction costs produced by the game of federal grantsmanship and by the related attempt of federal bureaucracies to initiate, control, and evaluate urban programs from Washington. But it is not clear as yet that revenue sharing has increased the competence and coherence of urban policy making. In fact revenue sharing has, if anything, increased the street fight between competing interests because it has served to make available a large amount of federal money at the local level.[1] At the same time higher-level government has either clearly specified what is an acceptable city expenditure or clearly left the determination of what is acceptable to local governments. The result is that to a surprising degree intergovernmental policy making remains, from the city's perspective, government by federal guideline, regulation, and evaluation, involving a continuous process, proposal writing, report writing, and requests for variances and exceptions.

These three concerns do not tell us in any precise way what programs and policies cities should emphasize, which they should contract, and which they should terminate. But they do provide criteria for assessing solutions offered now and in the past to the city's persistent problem of governance and control.

Historically two sorts of solutions have repeatedly been offered for the governance problem, and their own past failings do not prevent them from being offered again today. One solution is that of the scientific manager or business efficiency expert who says that if only tight managerial controls were imposed on city spending and if business techniques were introduced into the daily administration of city government, many urban problems would be resolved. There is some truth and considerable illusion in this view. The truth is that with any increase in accounting rigor or centralized management control, sloppy spending practices could and would be reduced. This is obviously a highly desirable result, but it is important to note at the same time that the thrust of the efficiency solution is essentially negative—that is, the logic of this solution, whether manifest in the form of council manager or in New York's Municipal Assistance Corporation, is to prevent wasteful spending and to avoid corruption. As such, the solution does not address the city's problems in meeting its positive goals such as delivering services responsively or creating an effective trust relationship between citizens and public employees.

If city government is on the brink of bankruptcy, the efficiency solution, even if negative, cannot be lightly dismissed, for it is hard to see how city hall can improve its responsiveness and increase trust if it cannot meet the payroll. So the use of an emergency control board in New York to keep the fiscal lid on may be a necessary condition of the present survival and future viability of urban government. After stringent business management techniques have been introduced in the area of fiscal control (and even if they are successful), the basic task of making city government work will remain, and we must find positive solutions to these problems of responsiveness, trust, regulation, and restructuring.

The introduction of business management techniques in city government has had its clear costs as well as its benefits. When an earlier generation of reformers set out to make city government run efficiently, they chose strategies designed to get politics out of the business of urban management. One such strategy was the creation of independent boards and commissions divorced from the street fight of urban politics, which would therefore operate an urban function more rationally and efficiently in the style of those large-scale business organizations so greatly admired by the reformers of the period. A second strategy involved the appointment of a city manager to be the central administrative officer and to act not as a politician but as a business manager. The cost of these strategies, and particularly of the boards and commissions, was that they made city government more remote and unaccountable. Democratic control and participation were sacrificed for efficient management. Seen in this light, it is not surprising that in the last two decades, movements for decentralization and citizen participation arose in reaction against the perceived bureaucratic rigidity and inaccessibility of these instruments of strongly centralized management.

A second enduring solution to the problem of urban governance is that of the professional bureaucrat who says that if only urban bureaucracies were strongly centralized under the control of service professionals and operated according to professional principles and practices, the disorder and inefficiency of street-level service delivery would be remedied. The strategy of professionalism shares with the efficient management solution the desire to remove politics from urban administration. But in this case it is the professional policemen, administrators, school superintendents, and social workers who are the beneficiaries of highly centralized administration. There is no doubt that increasing the professionalism of policemen, teachers, firemen, and social workers has produced significant benefits for urban service delivery. At least that is the indication if one compares modern-day policemen or firemen with the disorganized corps of volunteer firemen or the untrained policemen of the night watch. Despite these gains, the strategy of professionalism in service bureaucracies simply has not produced the rational, well-ordered system of service delivery that the advocates of professionalism envisioned. For all the centralized administration—the specialized police bureaucracies and the assistant school superintendents—as well as the training programs, promotion tests, procedures, and regulations, services at the street level do not appear to be delivered noticeably more responsively, coherently, or efficiently. At the same time the strategy of professionalism carried with it the same kinds of costs as the business management strategy, for professionalism, with its attendant centralization of service bureaucracy, created a greater physical and social distance between citizens and urban administrators and produced a cumbersome central bureaucratic structure.

The fact that many thoughtful observers of urban government have viewed (and continue to view) the strategy of efficient business management and the strategy of professionalism as potent remedies for the city's problem of governance invites (and even compels) a careful reexamination of the way we think about our cities as political, social, and economic organizations.

The two strategies discussed here are eminently plausible and even desirable. (It is hard to be against efficiency and professionalism in principle). It seems that these strategies should work—at least better than they have. The question is: What is it about the city that causes these strategies to be less successful than their proponents hoped would be the case? An even trickier question is: Would we want the kind of city government in which these strategies work easily?

In terms of the criteria of assessment presented, the trouble with both strategies is that while they address the problems created by decentralization (and especially fragmentation), they do not address the equally important problems created by centralization. In that sense, according to our analysis, these solutions provide only half a loaf. Neither strategy is designed to decrease the overload of demands on city hall, and the strategy of professionalism may indeed increase that load if, as is so often the case, professionals work to expand programs and policies in the areas of their expertise.

But the matter goes deeper than that. Both strategies are based on wishful notions of what city government and politics are like or would be like if only the right policies were pursued. The efficiency strategy makes sense in a world where there are fairly clear goals, rules of conduct, and divisions of responsibility; a fairly clear definition of inputs and outputs; and most important a reasonably clear understanding of what kinds of inputs (such as fiscal resources or manpower) produce what kinds of outputs (such as better schooling or police protection). Otherwise the efficiency strategy must inevitably reduce to cost cutting, and that is a slightly less compelling strategy than one that says city government can be both more efficient and more effective (could expand services, deliver them more responsively, and so forth) if it introduced certain management controls. The problem is that city government does not resemble the world of the efficiency analyst. Responsibility for service delivery is inherently divided (given the interactions between different services), and it is inherently hard to establish firm rules of conduct given the personal and discretionary character of the street-level service relationship. More important it is difficult to specify with any precision the actual (or desired) outputs of service delivery given the great diversity of demands, values, and

preferences that citizens and public employees alike articulate in
their appraisal of city services.

In many areas of service delivery there is no clear technology or
production function to indicate that the allocation of x resources
would produce y impact on a problem. That being the case, to ask
whether a particular service expenditure is efficient requires another deflating question: Compared to what? Also, if we knew that
upgrading the training or status of a policeman or paying him a
certain amount more would lead to a discernible change in police
protection, then the strategy of professionalism could be put on a
more solid foundation. It is for these reasons that the use of productivity measures in city government are relatively effective if we
are talking simply about the productivity of garbagemen measured
in terms of tons of garbage collected. But the productivity measures are less useful in talking about the productivity of teachers,
policemen, and social workers, and they are even less useful if we
really want to know whether the streets are cleaner or whether the
schools are more effective. A different way of making this point is
to say that the city's weak control system reflects not only government failings but also the crucial fact that so many forces and problems impinging on the city are beyond the direct control of city
hall.

In addition the mayor and other administrators in city hall must
always devise policies to deal with these elusive problems lacking
control over a great number of political actors and bureaucratic
organizations that operate within their domain. Among this number are neighborhood groups pressing for demands on city hall,
the various street-level governments (and their foot soldiers), the
independent boards, commissions, and authorities, and, most important, the federal and state governments who have made city
hall the agent for numerous service programs but who retain substantial control over the governance of those programs.

The city is an open system—open to problems coming from
many different sources (including sources outside the city) and
open to the involvement of many different would-be policy makers, most of whom are beyond the direct control of city hall. The
point is that because the city as an organization has such weak
boundaries, it is not easy to construct simple, clear, organizational

goals and strategies, and this makes the city an inhospitable environment for both the efficiency expert and the professional. So many ingredients have been mixed into the pot of urban problems and policy making that it is virtually impossible to transform the city into the kind of stable, tightly organized, hierarchical organization in which efficiency experts and service professionals would flourish.

The solutions we have been considering are frustrated by the fact that the city is not only a management and policy-making system; it is also a democratic institution. As a service delivery mechanism, good management would seem to be the main imperative of city government. But as a street-level government, that government in the American system closest to its citizens, good democratic procedure is also an imperative. In the end good management and good democracy must go hand in hand because of the nature of urban service delivery; it is difficult to be responsive to the diverse claims of urban residents if democratic processes are not working to represent the views and complaints of citizens and if there are few opportunities for citizen participation and evaluation in urban administration.

At the same time it would be naive to believe that there are no conflicts and trade-offs between the goals of good management and good democracy. In fact my point has been that the strategies of efficient business management and professionalism have pursued the first goal at the expense of the second, producing in the 1960s a strong citizen reaction against centralized bureaucratic control.

There is no obvious solution to the problem of urban government, only a number of competing perspectives and policy solutions. But the current discussion may be usefully simplified by isolating three perspectives on urban governance: community, city hall, and the structure of American federalism. Each of these perspectives leads to a very different perception of what is wrong with the city and what might be done about it. From the perspective of the community the city problem is about poor services, unresponsive bureaucracies, insensitive policemen or teachers, racial and neighborhood conflicts, and a general sense that city hall is extremely remote from the neighborhoods. To policy makers in city hall the urban problem looks quite different. It is a problem of fragmented bureaucracies, weak control over public employees, and a weak management structure—all in a context of increasing community demands for service. For the mayor and others in city hall the problem is one of political and administrative overload—an overload further compounded by the burdens of administering state and federal policies under conditions of fiscal stringency. From the perspective of the federal government, the city problem appears to be a product of fragmented and overlapping governmental jurisdictions and a proliferation of competing but confusingly intertwined bureaucratic organizations, inequality in resource allocation, weak implementation and coordination in intergovernmental policy making, weak regulation and evaluation of program performance, lack of clear responsibility and accountability for intergovernmental programs, and a lack of public planning either at a national level or the local level.

Thus from the community perspective problems of responsiveness in service delivery and mutual trust between the servers and the served appear to be dominant. At city hall the central problems appear to be achieving administrative and fiscal control and also maintaining political viability in the face of an increasingly overburdened policy-making system. From the federal perspective the central problems involve resource allocation, regulation of existing public policies, and the problem of restructuring the federal system itself to make it a more effective instrument of national policy making.

The crucial point is that in fundamental ways these perspectives are in conflict. Giving greater power to communities is likely to be seen in city hall as a strategy for increasing the fragmentation of city government. The authority and control of state and national government will often be in conflict with the authority of city hall. It is hard to increase the authority of the one without diminishing that of the other.

Now it is, of course, possible to imagine that in some ways the three perspectives may also be complementary. For example if both neighborhoods and higher-level governments were given increased amounts of control over urban policy making, this would seem to be a plausible way to reduce the overload on city hall. On balance, though, we must always keep in mind that the conflicts between the perspectives of community, city hall, and federalism are deeply rooted and will not suddenly go away.

Still this is not quite satisfying as a conclusion. It would be better to say something more to practicing community leaders, mayors, and higher-level executives about the problems and possibilities of policy making in the city government. In fact I believe that the argument of this book provides a number of simple clues about the nature of effective leadership and policy making in the urban arena.

The strongest implication for community leaders is that although it is easy to argue a negative case for decentralization, one should be very cautious of the opposite conclusion—that if communities were left alone they would develop a coherent and viable form of neighborhood government. If my analysis is correct the same features of street-fighting pluralism that make urban governance difficult will operate to make neighborhood government equally difficult if the goal is to replace a divided city community with a harmonious neighborhood unit.

There are two central implications for city hall policy makers. The first is to avoid political and administrative overload, and the way to do that is to focus sharply on basic services. In this sense "less" may indeed by "more." The second implication is that an urban policy maker who is sensitive to the great variety of urban problems and policy contexts and who can develop a range of strategies and responses suitable to the particular problem will do better than a policy maker who lacks a subtle understanding of the variability, uncertainty, and instability of urban governance. In practical terms this translates into a recommendation that central policy makers carefully distinguish the different kinds of problem and policy contexts they face; realize that they must develop a large repertoire of governance strategies; and then hand tailor these strategies to particular problems and policy contexts as they arise.

For higher-level executives the message of this book is less apparent. At present the structure of American federalism is in flux, and the shape of federal policy making thus is highly uncertain.

This means that there is now, as there always has been, a rich opportunity for redesign in the American system.

As a final note it seems likely that the large American city, in its present governmental form—with a city hall–dominated approach to policy making and management—may be becoming a political dinosaur, an evolutionary form that was once functional but now is increasingly out of phase with its political, economic, and social environment.

My thought is that we might well understand American city government as a late nineteenth-century adaptation to the pressures of urbanization and immigration. A city organized around a dominant (some would say "imperial") city hall was a viable way to tie together the many small neighborhoods on which the city was built, build the physical infrastructure of traction, parks, and other public works, and provide services to a rapidly growing urban population. The earlier governmental form—the small village or neighborhood—was plainly not capable of providing modern public works and services such as organized police and fire services, water supply, and transportation. So the city incorporated small villages, and city hall became the nerve center of a new and larger political community.

Milton Kotler illustrates this historical point vividly: "Germantown originated as a chartered town of Quaker immigrants, founded concurrently with Philadelphia to its south. Germantown continued as a political unit until it was annexed by Philadelphia without the consent of its residents in the consolidation of 1854. After 171 years of independent growth, that neighborhood lost its political self-rule. . . . In 1854, twenty-eight cities, towns, and boroughs lost their local government and were incorporated into the city of Philadelphia. The present day neighborhoods of Philadelphia can be traced to these original political units."[2]

Today the evolutionary forces that once made possible the rise of a city hall–based form of governance seem to be working against city hall. On the one hand urban policy problems constantly spill over city boundaries; many urban problems are really metropolitan, regional, statewide, or national problems. In addition the centrality and integrity of city hall as a policy-making system have been progressively undermined by the increased involvement of state and national government in urban affairs. On the other hand city hall's relationship to its neighborhood has become increasingly problematic as neighborhood groups complain that city hall is unresponsive or insensitive to street-level concerns. There has thus been an evolutionary increase in the concern for both neighborhood-level and higher-level policy making, and city hall is caught squarely in the middle of these evolutionary forces. City hall is obviously too large to be a viable neighborhood government and too small to make urban policy in the state and national arenas beyond city limits. This then is the nature of the evolutionary problem for city hall. It is not certain that city government is or must become a political dinosaur as a result of these forces; but the present line of evolution in urban policy making poses increasingly severe difficulties for mayors and their city governments.

Postscript:
The City in American Federalism

Up to this point I have treated the city as if it were a largely self-contained system. In truth the city is distinctive, but it is surely not self-contained. Thus it must be viewed as an abiding and central problem in American federalism. Compared with the efforts to improve the street-level service relationship and city hall management techniques, the structure of federalism has long been the most inviting and susceptible target for the redesign and restructuring of the American policy-making system as it impinges on urban problems. Many urban services are delivered today in much the same way they were twenty-five, fifty, or even one hundred years ago, and city hall has persisted in governing with a primitive management system (despite occasional waves of scientific management reform). But the federal system has been highly adaptive to the new problems and public designs. Moreover not only has the structure of federalism changed rapidly over time, but different parts of the structure have demonstrated a capacity to shift intergovernmental arrangements to deal with different kinds of pressures and problems. Consider, for example, the structural creativity of the broad range of federal programs: TVA, model cities, the Appalachian Regional Commission, community control of schools, community health centers, and the new regional health structure. Consider too the various forms of intergovernmental financing that have been used in different times and places in America: municipal bonds, housing subsidies, grants-in-aid, mandated spending programs, and revenue sharing.

Thus federalism has traditionally been a rich and powerful force because the design of federalism allows for flexible policy making, and the restructuring of financial and govermental arrangements goes to the heart of many (but by no means all) of the city's most pressing problems.

The Shape of American Federalism

Before considering how best the federal structure can adapt to fit the needs of cities in the late 1970s and 1980s, it might be wise to review current federal arrangements and their appropriateness to the problems suggested by the perspectives of community, city hall, and federalism.

The earliest and most primitive model of federalism is that of dual federalism, in which the functions of the national government and states are sharply separated. The two realms of national and local government have their own separate policy spheres and powers; they are, to use Morton Grodzins's famous metaphor, like the different layers in a layer cake.[1] The evidence for the accuracy of this model is found both in a historical concern for states' rights and local self-determination and in a legalistic concern that the powers and jurisdiction of governments on different levels be sharply defined. Needless to say, as Grodzins and Daniel Elazar have shown persuasively, layer-cake federalism has not been descriptive of American government for a long time.[2] Such rigidly divided powers and functions hardly suit modern social and urban policies. If the federal government and the states are to work together in education, welfare, or criminal justice, they are inevitably going to get involved with one another's programs and jurisdiction.

If the model of divided powers and functions is inadequate, what alternative model more accurately portrays the American system? According to Grodzins and Elazar, the model of shared powers and functions (or "marble-cake" federalism) provides both an accurate portrayal and presumably too a desired state of partnership between different levels of government.[3] Unlike the divided-powers model, the notion of marble-cake federalism is undoubtedly more realistic. But its desirability, relative to all possible federal arrangements, is not self-evident. On the one hand it is hard to be against cooperation and partnership if the opposite is rancor and conflict. On the other the recent experience of cities suggests that the shared-powers model creates a funnel effect in which the benevolent funds, programs, and regulations of higher-level governments, when funneled through the intergovernmental system, dump a tremendous number of administrative and financial burdens onto city governments. The logic of this objection is that most social policies turn out to be urban policies and, as such, they can make a difference only if they are implemented effectively at the street level—in the classroom or on the police beat. Thus social policies decided at a higher level inevitably require for their implementation extensive administrative machinery, as well as continuing evaluation and fiscal control at the street level. In this sense, we might say that the federal and state governments come up with the ideas; the cities get the programs.

Curiously, a common feature of both the layer cake and marble-cake models is that neither is particularly concerned with problems of responsiveness and trust at the street level; neither is much concerned with managerial efficiency or political viability in city hall, and the concern for an effective intergovernmental policy-making system is limited to the argument that the partnership of the marble-cake model is, for good and obvious reasons, superior to the policy segregation and implicit conflict of the layer-cake version. To find models of federalism that bear directly on the concerns at city hall and in the community, we must look at two more recent models of federalism—the grants-in-aid model and the community action-model cities model.[4]

Grants-in-Aid: Ordeal by Paper

The most pervasive federal arrangement before the onset of revenue sharing is that of federal grants-in-aid. The federal government becomes a kind of public banker with certain desirable projects in mind, and localities become financially dependent "firms" seeking new sources of capital investment. The grant-in-aid model gives great power to the federal government, which plays the banker role, but it is not without benefits to certain local bureaucracies. For the fortunate local "grantsmen" who persuade the federal government to invest in their cities, grants can provide powerful political weapons, as the regimes of New Haven's Richard C. Lee and Chicago's Richard Daley have shown quite clearly. But the grant system had several major defects. From the community point of view the relationship that grants fostered between the federal and local experts in the renewal and social service bureaucracies was not conducive—to say the least—to greater community participation and greater attention to street-level needs. Under the system the local experts' major constituency and audience was the federal government, not neighborhood interests. Further, the grants system served to increase the instability and uncertainty of urban management in city hall. It was inherent in the grantsmanship game that urban policy makers never knew from one year to another how much money they would have in the next year's budget (and they were forced to spend a great deal of their administrative energies getting or keeping federal grants). From the federal perspective the grant system was even more problematic. It produced an administrative ordeal for many of those involved, it required detailed program specifications, massive grant proposals, and continued monitoring and evaluation. It used to be a joke in city halls across the country that by the time the locality finished answering all the questions of the federal government and supplying all needed information, the grant proposal had to be delivered to the appropriate agency in a wheelbarrow.

In addition to these administrative costs the grant relationship also produced more tension between the national government and local governments. As Jeffrey Pressman has convincingly demonstrated, the administrative interests and incentives of the national partner in a grant-in-aid relationship are diametrically opposed to the administrative interests and incentives of the local partner.[5] That is, the national government usually wants to maintain strong control over programs, make only short-term financial commitments, and launch ambitious and far-reaching programs. By contrast the local recipient of aid wants autonomy over its funded programs, stable long-term funding, and limited program objectives that will make local administrators look capable (not foolish for having inflated aspirations).

One of Pressman's major conclusions is that given these very different interests and incentives, there is no reason to expect the national and local governments to cooperate enthusiastically. This view calls into serious question the faith of Grodzins and Elazar that shared powers inevitably mean partnership or cooperation. Pressman's suggestion is that having widely shared, deeply intertwined functions (as in the grant relationship) can lead not to cooperation but to enduring institutional conflict.

Unilateral Intervention

Lyndon Johnson's war on poverty produced a quite different approach to federalism. Here the national government sought to intervene directly in the governance of cities by stimulating citizen participation and direct problem solving at the community level. There is no point in recounting here the myriad political and administrative difficulties produced by these experiments in federalism. What is worth noting is that viewed from the three perspectives of the community, city hall, and federalism, we can see the inherent conflicts and trade-offs in these federal policy instruments. To the extent that community action and model cities actually met the problems felt in the community by fostering participation and new decentralized service mechanisms, the programs were likely to alienate policy makers in city hall. From the city hall perspective it seemed that federal dollars were being spent deliberately to increase administrative overload, to organize protests against local governments, and to develop "paragovernments," which further fragmented urban government. On the other hand, to the extent that city hall was able to control the community action and model cities programs, this form of federalism seemed entirely bankrupt from the community viewpoint. Finally, as far as strengthening the federal system is concerned, community action had the consequence of increasing the amount and intensity of conflict between different levels of government over the control and direction of the two programs.

Metropolitan Government

Another historical model of how American federalism might be structured to solve urban problems involves the creation of new units of metropolitan or regional government. For generations urban reformers have urged the adoption of metropolitan or regional governments to bring political jurisdictions in line with existing social and economic communities. But for all their urgings, metro governments, such as those in Miami, Nashville, Indianapolis, and Minneapolis, remain curiosities.[7] They constitute an idea whose time is constantly said to have come but whose acceptance is rare. A central problem with metropolitan solutions is that their benefits and costs look very different from the three perspectives. From the community perspective metro government looks suspicious, if not dangerous. Small neighborhoods and especially minority communities worry that their place and power would be greatly diluted in a larger political community. And metro government seems to be exactly the wrong answer to the city's administrative problems, for any solutions it comes up with would inevitably move the center of government farther away from street-level problems (rather than bringing government closer to the neighborhood).

From the city hall perspective metropolitan solutions present an extreme solution to the problem of administrative overload, since city hall would have its management problems removed at the cost of losing many, if not all, of its powers and responsibilities. In fact city officials in metro Miami and elsewhere have often fought to maintain their political power and administrative responsibility and, in so doing, have caused persistent and damaging conflicts within their metropolitan governments.[8]

Significantly it is only in the perspective of federalism that metropolitan and regional solutions seem to be beneficial. These larger governmental units have the virtues of rationalizing fragmented and overlapping governmental jurisdictions, creating more equitable and efficient taxing and spending mechanisms, and producing economies of scale in service delivery.

In sum, the fact that metropolitan solutions satisfy the perceived needs of only one level of government is a major reason why metropolitan government rarely appears in American federalism.

Reactive, Buck-Passing, and Free Market Federalism

The models discussed so far cover most of the major structural patterns and planned reorganizations in the recent history of American federalism. However there are three other patterns to keep in mind that reveal recurrent failings in American federalism —failings that a new and better intergovernmental system should be designed to avoid.

The first is found in the tendency of higher-level governments to deal with urban problems only after they have reached crisis proportions. According to Mark Gelfand, whatever the design of American federalism, the intergovernmental structure has mobilized to give substantial support to the city only in emergencies.[9]

The failing can best be described as a reflection of reactive decision making.

The second failing, which I term the "buck-passing syndrome," exists when policy makers at different levels of government spend their time trying to pin the blame for the city's problems on some other government. Buck-passing federalism describes the familiar phenomena of mayors blaming governors for failing to give adequate resources to the city, governors passing the blame to Washington, and Washington blaming the mayors for being careless administrators and wasteful spenders.

At first glance this buck-passing pattern might seem to reflect nothing more than a natural political impulse, and indeed the pattern is deeply rooted in the structure of American federalism. My argument is that, given the multiplicity of governmental units, each seeking a relatively stable and secure stock of powers and fiscal resources, intergovernmental relations in America are inherently competitive. More concretely, governmental units in a federal system follow a commonsense principle that must inevitably produce continual conflict between different levels of governments. The basic principle is to retain (or increase) the benefits of governmental power while minimizing the costs of public action. This principle may sound simpleminded, but its consequences are anything but trivial. If each government acts to maintain (or expand) its power and policy domain and also to reduce the financial costs of doing so, the only possibile strategy is to seek money from another level of government and, if unsuccessful, to blame one's difficulties on the other level. The corollary of this pattern is that when a donor seeks some increased power and involvement in a particular policy arena by virtue of its fiscal contribution, intense conflicts over authority and control will inevitably result as a consequence of the power-maintenance principle.

Thus American federalism tends to produce continual conflict and competition. If governments look for but do not find added resources elsewhere, they are almost certain to resort to buck passing. Even if governments are successful in getting money from outside sources, competition will intensify when the donor government asserts its own power claims.

There are at least two possible ways out of this seemingly inevitable conflict syndrome. One is that the donor government will give
money away without any reciprocal claims to power and involvement (which is the stated claim of revenue sharing). The second is
to define public problems in other than financial terms, in this way
avoiding the beggar-donor relationship. Significantly this is the implication of the current "less-is-more" view, which says that urban
governments can reduce their economic and administrative costs
dramatically by attacking fewer problems (and performing fewer
functions) more intensively.

Buck-passing federalism is, in essence, a manifestation of vertical, political competition in American government. However,
there is also a pattern of horizontal competition that has serious
negative consequences for the American system as a whole. This
pattern can be termed free market competition—horizontal competition between similar local jurisdictions, state against state, city
against city, and suburb against suburb. This pattern is expressed
in competition between communities to protect their social and
economic assets at the same time that they try to avoid incurring
any new social and economic burdens. More concretely, the pattern is manifest in exclusionary zoning and fiscal zoning, which
together constitute the following competitive maxim: attract high-
income households and clean industries, keep out low-income
households and dirty industry. I call this "free market" competition because the present structure of American federalism permits
localities to act like relatively autonomous "firms," each seeking
profitable industries and residents and avoiding unprofitable
ones. Interestingly the idea of free market choice and competition
between jurisdictions has been strongly defended by an econo-
mist, Charles Tiebout, who argues that the present structure of
autonomous, fragmented local jurisdictions provides consumers
with many different bundles of housing stock, public services, and
other amenities and that these diverse community products reflect
diverse consumer preferences and permit wide consumer choice.[10]
Tiebout's argument makes some sense if we are talking about a set
of relatively affluent suburbs that differ largely in their amenities
and life-style characteristics. But viewed from the perspective of
the city, Tiebout's argument is a recipe for certain disaster because

most cities simply cannot compete with most suburbs for fiscally profitable residence and industries. Certainly it is a plain fact of present urban life that the cities have been losing their assets and incurring liabilities at a rapid rate. Because of their fiscal structures and service obligations, cities cannot compete (or even survive) in a system of free market federalism.

National Dominance

In many countries, particularly in those with a unitary form of government, the national government plays such a dominant role in urban policy making that it is fair to say that the city is governed directly by the central government. In France, for example, the mayor is by law an administrative agent of the national government. In Great Britain the national government has acted directly to restructure the management system of city government; and more significantly a royal commission has brought about the complete reordering of the geographical boundaries and governmental structure of government in relation to cities. The national government created a metropolitan government with a two-tier structure: a single government council for the metropolitan area as a whole and a series of smaller councils concerned with neighborhood-level service delivery. In addition in many European democracies, housing, educational, and welfare policies are formulated, legislated, and implemented by the national government. Thus urban policies are national policies, and the city government becomes the administrative custodian of national programs and policies.

Many observers of American city government look with admiration and envy at the national dominance model and suggest that what American cities really need is a national urban system run with the resources and planning strengths of the central government. There is a good deal to be said for increasing the national involvement in certain urban policy arenas, but the model of national dominance is neither politically feasible nor entirely desirable.

In terms of political feasibility, the model of national dominance would require the virtual destruction of the present system of

American federalism. For the central government to run a full-fledged national urban policy, it would have to have clear authority over both states and city governments, and this is unlikely to happen as long as there are governors, mayors, and a written constitution.

More important, the model of national dominance does not answer (or even address) all the crucial problems suggested in the three perspectives. From the perspective of community, putting the federal government in charge of urban governments increases the distance between governments and the neighborhood and makes it all the more unlikely that policy will be carefully tailored to reflect neighborhood variations.

From the perspective of city hall the model of national dominance might have the virtue of reducing the administrative overload in the city government (if the federal government took over a great deal of administrative responsibility as well as planning and financing). But it is more likely, from the experience in Western Europe, that the city would remain the administrative custodian of national policies. If this were the case the twin problems of how to reduce administrative overload and increase managerial control and efficiency would remain unchanged.

The strong argument for the model of national dominance is, of course, that the federal government has a far greater taxing capacity than state or local governments and therefore has a distinct advantage as a banker in American policy making. Having the federal government play the banker role for urban programs would presumably relieve the fiscal pressures and constraints that are placed on city governments with their reliance on property taxes. A second related advantage is that the federal government has a far greater capacity to distribute money equally across local jurisdictions and thereby reduce the fiscal imbalance between local communities—an imbalance that virtually every student points to as a fundamental flaw of American government. A third advantage (which is self-evident) is that only the federal government can provide regional or national planning in policy areas where government is providing large-scale public goods whose impacts, by definition, extend beyond local jurisdiction.

State Initiative

For many years state governments have been the silent partners in American federalism.[11] States were slow to respond to urban problems in the 1960s if they were not overtly hostile to the cities themselves. In recent years, however, some state governments have begun to play a far more active role in urban issues and problem solving as they have become increasingly engaged in housing, education, environmental protection, and other social service policies. Indeed some states have created departments of consumer affairs, departments of environmental protection, and city-oriented housing authorities, such as the ill-fated New York Urban Development Corporation. With this apparent resurgence of the states, which was certainly stimulated by revenue sharing, it now becomes possible to imagine that state governments might provide a powerful solution to urban problems by taking over the financing and administration of significant urban functions. State governments might even exercise strict fiscal and administrative control over urban government, as the state of New York has been forced to do in the face of New York City's impending bankruptcy. And it is important to remember that city governments are now, as they always have been, legal creatures of the state, and it remains possible in principle for the states to take back power and functions delegated to the cities under home-rule legislation.

The benefits and costs of state initiative in urban government turn out to parallel rather closely the benefits and costs of national dominance. From the perspective of community, increased state initiative (or direct takeover) might again seem to be a move in the wrong direction since it would also move governmental decision making farther away from the neighborhood. The obvious argument for state initiative is that state governments have greater fiscal capacities and a wider tax catchment area than city governments, and thus state financing of urban programs, in principle, should be able to reduce the fiscal pressures on urban government and at the same time level out the fiscal imbalances caused by the present taxing and spending system in local jurisdictions. The important difference between national dominance and state initiative comes from the perspective of city hall. Whereas it is likely to be difficult for the federal government to assume day-to-day management responsibilities in the city and thereby reduce the overload on city hall, it should be far easier for state governments to do so because of their proximity and their existing legal powers and administrative involvements. A useful question in this context is whether the state government of New York, through the Municipal Assistence Corporation and the Emergency Financial Control Board, has been able to assume operating responsibilities effectively in important areas of city management. I believe the answer is yes, but it is obviously too soon to make a confident appraisal.

Revenue Sharing

The most significant new model in American federalism is found in the revenue-sharing program of the newest new federalism.[12] It is still premature to evaluate the impact and potential of revenue sharing, but I think it is possible to put this new solution in perspective by appraising it in terms of its ability to meet the problems evoked in our three perspectives. But first one preliminary distinction is called for. To the extent that revenue sharing alters the relationship between the city and the federal government and creates new rules in urban policy making, further appraisal is called for. Understood in this way, the question becomes: What happens to city government when urban policy makers are given greater discretion in spending money that was once available only in categorical grant programs? Let us consider this question from our three perspectives. First, from the perspective of community there is no evidence that revenue sharing increases citizen participation or the city's attention to street-level service problems. In fact citizen participation requirements on revenue sharing are generally weak, and many neighborhood groups feel the absence of federal programs targeted directly at their concerns and requiring participation (as in community action and model cities).

Second, from the perspective of city hall, revenue sharing may, if anything, increase the administrative overload in city hall rather than reduce it because city hall spending decisions are far less restricted and virtually every urban group can stake a claim for a share of the money. By contrast, under the categorical grant system, city hall could fend off demands for money by local groups by saying that federal regulations and guidelines kept them from granting it (thereby passing the blame). Indeed as a participant in the process of allocating revenue-sharing money in New Haven, and having watched the process in other cities, my suspicion is that the new solution of revenue sharing strips city hall policy makers of significant political and administrative protection and leaves them holding a financial grab-bag, causing an increase in the ratio of enemies made to friends acquired in every decision.

Finally, from the perspective of the structure of federalism, revenue sharing may or may not solve the central administrative problem of paperwork and other red tape produced by the grant-in-aid relationship (with the wheelbarrows of proposed documents and evaluations). At least that was one of the main reasons that the Nixon administration gave for moving toward revenue sharing. However if the federal government does not make clear its eligibility requirements and other guidelines in special revenue-sharing programs, city government may still be caught up in a continual process of administrative clearance and guideline changes that undermines the good intentions of new federalism. Moreover revenue sharing will never by itself constitute a coherent national urban policy in which broad national interests as well as local interests are taken carefully into account. If anything, local interests are emphasized at the expense of national programs. And this, of course, is not accidental. It is an intended consequence of the philosophy of home rule found in revenue sharing.

A Hybrid Solution

The burden of my argument so far is that none of the available solutions meets the perceived deficiencies of urban government. Rather it seems that any viable intergovernmental solution to the urban problem must involve elements of both centralization and decentralization.

From the community perspective, the only way to deal with neighborhood variations—and with the special problems of trust and responsiveness in service delivery—is to decentralize government and increase the role and powers of neighborhood-level institutions (both community organizations and street-level bureaucracies). Just as important, from the perspective of the federal government, it would seem equally clear that the only way to increase the fiscal resources being applied to problems and to achieve greater equity in resource allocation is to move toward a more centralized government and to increase federal-state responsibility for the banker's role. To the extent that one is worried about simple incompetence in urban administration, increased state control appears to be at least a plausible line of solution.

Finally, from the city hall perspective, this hybrid solution of centralization and decentralization would appear to go to the heart of the problem of administrative overload. If some of the city's operating, planning, and financing responsibilities were taken over by the state and national governments, the burden on city hall should be greatly relieved. Which functions should be pushed up and which down? Here it is enough to offer some simple clues. Services with a strong neighborhood impact (like police, fire, and education) are obvious candidates for decentralized administration. Problems that are inherently resource problems or ones that involve major equity issues (transportation, housing, welfare, and educational financing) are obvious candidates for delegation to higher-level government.

The result of such a hybrid solution would tend to divide responsibility for policy areas (sanitation versus welfare) as well as government functions (the banking versus the day-to-day administrative functions). As such the hybrid solution might appear to be a throwback to the earlier model of divided power. Be that as it may, if my analysis of the three perspectives is correct, the hybrid solution provides the most plausible approach available to the major problems of urban government.

Notes

Preface

1
Edward C. Banfield, *The Unheavenly City* (Boston: Little, Brown, 1968); Norton Long, *The Unwalled City* (New York: Basic Books, 1972).

2
Edward C. Banfield and James G. Wilson, *City Politics* (Cambridge: Harvard University Press, 1965).

Chapter 1

1
Charles O. Jones and Layne D. Hoppe, eds., *The Urban Crisis in America* (Washington, D.C.: Washington National Press, 1969), p. 3.

2
Ibid., p. 8.

3
Ibid., p. iii.

4
Michael Harrington, *The Other America* (New York: Macmillan, 1962).

5
See David Boesel and Peter H. Rossi, *Cities Under Siege* (New York: Basic Books, 1971).

6
For one review of these programs, see Sar Levitan, *The Great Society's Poor Law* (Baltimore: Johns Hopkins University Press, 1969).

7
Eli Ginzberg and Robert M. Solow, eds., *The Public Interest*, no. 34 (Winter 1974): 11.

8
All figures from the 1970 Census.

9
Banfield, *Unheavenly City*.

10
"Cities in Peril," *U.S. News and World Report*, April 7, 1975, p. 43.

11
Ibid., p. 46.

12
Robert B. Pettergill and Jogindar S. Uppal, *Can Cities Survive?* (New York: St. Martin's Press, 1974).

13
For a review of this experience, see Alice Rivlin, *Systematic Thinking for Social Action* (Washington, D.C.: The Brookings Institution, 1971).

For a latter-day, more critical account, see Richard R. Nelson, *The Moon and the Ghetto* (New York: W. W. Norton and Co., 1977).

14
James Bryce, *The American Commonwealth* (New York and London: Macmillan, 1888), 1:608.

15
For a vivid account of the careers of old-time bosses, see Ralph Martin, *The Bosses* (New York: Putnam, 1964).

16
Albert J. Reiss, Jr., "The Servers and the Served in Service," in J. Patrick Crecine, ed., *Financing the Metropolis*, Urban Affairs Annual Reviews, vol. 4 (1970), pp. 561–576.

17
This concept has been given powerful definition and elaboration in Michael Lipsky, "Toward a Theory of Street-Level Bureaucracy," in Willis Hawley and Michael Lipsky, eds., *Theoretical Perspectives in Urban Politics* (Englewood Cliffs, N.J.: Prentice-Hall, 1974), pp. 196–213.

18
Nathan Glazer and Daniel P. Moynihan, *Beyond the Melting Pot* (Cambridge: The MIT Press, 1963).

19
Robert Fogelson, *Fragmented Metropolis, Los Angeles* (Cambridge: Harvard University Press, 1967).

20
Wallace Sayre and Herbert Kaufman, *Governing New York City* (New York: Russell Sage Foundation, 1965).

21
Norton Long, "The Local Community as an Ecology of Games," in Norton Long, *The Polity* (Chicago: Rand McNally, 1962), pp. 139–155.

22
Robert Dahl, *Who Governs?* (New Haven: Yale University Press, 1961).

23
Ibid., pp. 200ff.

24
Ibid., pp. 215ff.

25
Floyd Hunter, *Community Power Structure.* (Chapel Hill: University of North Carolina Press, 1953).

26
Ibid.

27
For a compendium of many of these comparative approaches, see
Michael Aiken and Paul Mott, eds., *The Structure of Community Power*
(New York: Random House, 1970).

28
Oliver P. Williams and Charles R. Adrian, *Four Cities* (Philadelphia:
University of Pennsylvania Press, 1963), p. 34.

29
Ibid.

30
Terry N. Clark, *Community Structure and Decision Making* (San Francisco: Chandler, 1968).

31
Banfield and Wilson pay substantial attention to these categories in
City Politics. See chapters 9–13.

32
David Easton, *The Political System*, 2nd ed. (New York: Knopf, 1971).

33
Thomas Dye, *Politics, Economics, and the Public* (Chicago: Rand
McNally, 1966).

34
J. Patrick Crecine, *Government Problem Solving* (Chicago: Rand
McNally, 1969).

Chapter 2

1
See, for example, William A. Robson, *Local Government in Crisis* (London: George Allen and Unwin, 1966).

2
See Jeffrey L. Pressman, *Federal Programs and City Politics* (Berkeley:
University of California Press, 1975), p. 2.

3
Martha Derthick, *New Towns In-Town* (Washington, D.C.: The Urban
Institute, 1972).

4
Delos Wilcox, *The American City: A Problem in Democracy* (New York:
Macmillan Co., 1904), p. 28.

5
See Albert J. Reiss, Jr., *The Price and the Public* (New Haven: Yale
University Press, 1971), pp. 173–221.

6
I base this judgment on findings from a survey that was made in 1971 of 450 residents in three neighborhoods in New York City. The survey explored citizen attitudes in these neighborhoods toward the quality of service delivery and the desirability of neighborhood governments. This research forms a part of a larger study of services, delivery, and decentralization: Douglas Yates, *Neighborhood Democracy* (Lexington, Mass.: D. C. Heath, 1973).

7
Gerald Suttles, *The Social Order of the Slum* (Chicago: University of Chicago Press, 1968).

8
Sayre and Kaufman, *Governing New York City.*

9
Daniel Bell and Virginia Held, "The Community Revolution," *The Public Interest,* no. 16 (Summer 1969): 142–177.

10
Ibid., p. 142.

11
Ibid., p. 143.

12
Charles Adrian, "Leadership and Decision-Making in Major Cities," *Public Administration Review* 18 (Summer 1958): 212.

13
Betty Zisk, *Local Interest Politics* (New York: Bobbs-Merrill, 1973).

14
Charles B. Wheeler, *Doctor in Politics* (Kansas City: Inform, 1974), p. 198.

15
Henry W. Maier, *Challenge to the Cities* (New York: Random House, 1966), p. 14.

16
Stephen K. Bailey, "A Structured Interaction Pattern for Harpsichord and Kazoo," *Public Administration Review* 14 (Summer 1954): 204.

17
Carl B. Stokes, *Promises of Power* (New York: Simon and Schuster, 1973), p. 109.

18
John V. Lindsay, *The City* (New York: W. W. Norton, 1969), pp. 14–15.

19
For a vivid account of La Guardia's leadership style, see Erwin C. Hargrove, "The Drama of Reform," in J. D. Barber, ed., *Political Leader-*

ship in American Government (Boston: Little, Brown, 1964), pp. 94–117.

20
Maier, *Challenge,* p. 14.

21
Charles Hardin, *Presidential Power and Accountability* (Chicago: University of Chicago Press, 1974), p. 3.

22
Leonard I. Ruchelman, ed., *Big City Mayors* (Bloomington: University of Indiana Press, 1969), p. 3.

23
James Parton, "The Government of the City of New York," *North American Review* 102 (1866): 455–456.

24
Cited by Ruchelman, *Big City Mayors,* p. 301.

25
Nat Hentoff, *A Political Life: The Education of John V. Lindsay* (New York: Knopf, 1969), p. 82.

26
Ibid., p. 85.

27
In addition to Lipsky's analysis, see James Q. Wilson, *Varieties of Police Behavior* (Cambridge: Harvard University Press, 1968), p. 6.

28
C. E. Lindblom, *The Intelligence of Democracy* (New York: The Free Press, 1965).

29
Parton, "Government," pp. 455–456.

30
John V. Lindsay, *The City* (New York: Norton, 1969), p. 15.

31
Kenneth T. Palmer, *State Politics in the United States* (New York: St. Martin's Press, 1972), pp. 83ff.

32
See David Mayhew, *Congress: The Electoral Connection* (New Haven: Yale University Press, 1974), pp. 54ff.

Chapter 3

1
This chapter relies heavily on the following accounts and analyses of the development of urban service delivery. For an account of urban

services in the eighteenth century, see Carl Bridenbaugh, *Cities in Revolt: Urban Life in America, 1743–1776* (New York: Oxford University Press, 1955), chap. 1, and Ernest S. Griffith, *History of American City Government: The Colonial Period* (New York: Oxford University Press, 1936). For nineteenth-century perspectives on the slow rise of police, fire, garbage, health, educational, and related social services, see Ernest Griffith, *Modern Development of City Government* (London: Oxford University Press, 1927). See Ruben C. Bellan, *The Evolving City* (Toronto: Copp Clark Publishing Company, 1971); Charles Zeublin, *American Municipal Progress* (New York: Macmillan, 1919); Ernest S. Griffith, *Current Municipal Problems* (Cambridge, Mass.: The Riverside Press, 1933); and Arthur M. Schlesinger, *The Rise of the City* (New York: Macmillan, 1933). The character and development and changing patterns of urban public administration and service delivery are treated in vivid detail in a number of textbooks on municipal administration generally published after 1900 but that survey changing management practices in the city during the late nineteenth century. I have found the following textbooks particularly helpful in illuminating the origins of urban services: Henry G. Hodges, *City Management* (New York: Crofts and Co., 1939); John Fairlie, *Municipal Administration* (New York: Macmillan, 1901); Lent D. Upson, *Practice of Municipal Administration* (New York: The Century Co., 1926); Alfred Conkling, *City Government in the United States* (New York: The Century Co., 1904); Delos Wilcox, *The American City: A Problem in Democracy* (New York: Macmillan, 1904); and Frederic Howe, *The Modern City and Its Problems* (New York: Scribner's, 1915).

2
Ernest Griffith, *History of American City Government: The Colonial Period* (New York: Oxford University Press, 1936), p. 194.

3
A. Vidich and J. Bensman, *Small Town in Mass Society* (Garden City, N.Y.: Doubleday Anchor, 1960).

4
For a useful development of this point, see Seymour J. Mandelbaum, *Boss Tweed's New York* (New York: Wiley, 1965).

5
For argument along these lines, see Robert K. Merton, "The Latest Functions of the Machine," in Merton, *Social Theory and Social Structure* (New York: The Free Press, 1957), pp. 72, 88. For a comparative perspective on the centralizing role of political machines, see James Scott, *Comparative Political Corruption* (Englewood Cliffs, N.J.: Prentice-Hall, 1975).

6
See Edward Costikyan, *Behind Closed Doors* (New York: Harcourt Brace, 1968). The saga of George Washington Plunkitt is told in William L. Riordan, *Plunkitt of Tammany Hall* (New York: Dutton, 1963).

7
Fred I. Greenstein, *The American Party System and the American People* (Englewood Cliffs, N.J.: Prentice-Hall, 1963), p. 48.

8
The rise of federal involvement in urban affairs is ably analyzed in Roscoe C. Martin, *The Cities and the Federal System* (New York: Atherton Press, 1965).

9
David Rogers, *110 Livingston Street* (New York: Random House, 1968).

10
James Q. Wilson, ed., *Urban Renewal* (Cambridge, Mass.: The MIT Press, 1966).

11
The rise of New Haven's bureaucratic machine in the urban renewal sphere is examined with care in Phillip Singerman, unpublished manuscript, Yale University, 1975.

12
See Dahl, *Who Governs?* on the executive-centered condition in renewal. For a later account, see Raymond E. Wolfinger, *The Politics of Progress* (Englewood Cliffs, N.J.: Prentice-Hall, 1974), pp. 131–354.

13
Though flawed, the most interesting account of Moses's remarkable career is Robert A. Caro, *The Power Broker* (New York: Knopf, 1974).

14
J. Clarence Davies, *Neighborhood Groups and Urban Renewal* (New York: Columbia University Press, 1966).

15
Bell and Held, "Community Revolution."

16
This pattern is vividly portrayed in Michael Lipsky, *Protest in City Politics* (Chicago: Rand McNally, 1970).

17
See Daniel P. Moynihan, *Maximum Feasible Misunderstanding* (New York: The Free Press, 1969).

18
For a good account of the rise and fall of the model cities program, see Edward C. Banfield, "Making a New Federal Program: Model

Cities, 1964–68," in Allen P. Sindler, *Policy and Politics in America* (Boston: Little, Brown, 1973).

19
Reuben C. Bellan, *The Evolving City* (Vancouver: Coop Clark Publishing Company, 1971), p. 273.

20
For an account of the role of scavengers, see John Duffy, *A History of Public Health in New York City* (New York: Russell Sage Foundation, 1968), p. 185.

21
Jonathan Rubenstein, *City Police* (New York: Farrar, Straus and Giroux, 1973), p. 15.

22
Ibid.

23
Ibid., p. 17.

24
Mandelbaum, *Tweed's New York*, p. 55.

25
Henry G. Hodges, *City Management* (New York: F. S. Crofts and Company, 1939), p. 157.

26
The concept of mutual bargaining and adjustment is developed in meticulous detail in Lindblom, *Intelligence of Democracy*.

27
Mandelbaum, *Tweed's New York*, p. 50.

28
Bellan, *Evolving City*, p. 255.

29
John A. Fairlie, *Municipal Administration* (New York: Macmillan, 1901), p. 145.

30
Marvin Lazerson, *Origins of the Urban School* (Cambridge: Harvard University Press, 1971), p. 4.

31
Michael B. Katz, *Class, Bureaucracy, and Schools* (New York: Praeger, 1971), p. 68.

32
Ibid., p. 70.

33
Ibid., p. 69.

34
Ibid., p. 81.

35
Roy Lubove, *The Professional Altruist* (New York: Atheneum, 1969), p. 55.

36
Ibid., p. 161.

37
Banfield, *The City*, p. 20.

38
Charles N. Glaab and A. Theodore Brown, *A History of Urban America* (New York: Macmillan, 1967), p. 165.

39
Richard C. Wade, *The Urban Frontier* (Chicago: University of Chicago Press, 1959), p. 84.

40
Raymond N. Muhl, *Poverty in New York* (New York: Oxford University Press, 1971), p. 11.

41
Joseph Hawes, *Children in Urban Society* (New York: Oxford University Press, 1971), p. 95.

42
Lewis Yablonsky, *The Violent Gang* (Baltimore: Penguin, 1962), p. 108.

43
Herbert Ashbury, *The Gangs of New York* (New York: Knopf, 1927), p. 113.

44
Sam Bass Warner, Jr., *The Urban Wilderness* (New York: Harper & Row, 1972), pp. 202–203.

45
Carl Bridenbaugh, *Cities in Revolt* (New York: Oxford University Press, 1955), p. 301.

46
Constance McLaughlin Green, *The Role of Urban America* (New York: Harper & Row, 1965), p. 109.

47
Wade, *Urban Frontier*, p. 99.

48
Ibid., p. 92.

49
Green, *Urban America*, p. 111.

50
Wade, *Urban Frontier*, p. 89.

51
Duffy, *History of Public Health*, p. 141.

52
Green, *Urban America*, p. 120.

53
Ibid., p. 116.

54
Wade, *Urban Frontier*, p. 89.

55
Ibid.

56
Moses Rischin, *The Promised City* (New York: Harper & Row, 1970), p. 52.

57
Frank J. Goodnow, *City Government in the United States* (New York: The Century Co., 1904), p. 57.

58
Charles Zueblin, *American Municipal Progress* (New York: Macmillan, 1919), p. 108.

59
Ibid., pp. 35–36.

60
Ibid., p. 306.

61
Ibid., pp. 75–76.

62
John Gardiner and Olson, *Theft of the City* (Indianapolis: University of Indiana Press, 1974), p. 47.

63
Hodges, *City Management*, p. 501.

64
Colin Greer, *The Great School Legend* (New York: Basic Books, 1972), p. 108.

65
David F. Musto, *The American Disease* (New Haven: Yale University Press, 1973), p. 246.

66
Glaab and Brown, *Urban America* p. 162.

67
Frederic C. Howe, *The Modern City and Its Problems* (New York: Scribners: 1915), p. 307.

68
Katz, *Class, Bureaucracy*, p. 71.

69
Cited in Blanche Coll, *Perspectives in Public Welfare* (Washington, D.C.: HEW, 1969), p. 37.

70
Mohl, *Poverty*, p. 31.

71
Carl Kaestle, *The Evolution of an Urban School System* (Cambridge: Harvard University Press, 1973), p. 119.

72
Cited in Mohl, *Poverty*, p. 264.

73
Lawrence J. R. Herson, "The Lost World of Municipal Government," *American Political Science Review* 51 (1957): 330–345.

Chapter 4

1
Dahl, *Who Governs?*; Banfield, *Unheavenly City*.

2
Jeffrey Pressman and Aaron Wildavsky, *Implementation* (Berkeley: University of California Press, 1973).

3
Lindblom, *Intelligence of Democracy*.

4
C. E. Lindblom, "Bargaining: The Hidden Hand in Government," in *The Public Interest*.

5
The idea of nondecisions is developed in detail in Peter Bachnach and Morton S. Baratz, "Two Faces of Power," *American Political Science Review* 56 (December 1962): 949ff.

6
Lindblom, *Intelligence of Democracy*, and Aaron Wildavsky, *The Politics of the Budgetary Process* (Boston: Little, Brown, 1964).

7
Matthew A. Crenson, *The Unpolitics of Air Pollution* (Baltimore: Johns Hopkins University Press, 1971).

8
Jewel Bellush and Stephen David, *Race and Politics in New York City* (New York: Praeger: 1971), pp. 98–133.

9
Ibid., pp. 59–97.

10
Ibid.

11
Diana Gordon, *City Limits* (New York: Charterhouse, 1973), p. 282.

12
Ibid., pp. 17–62.

13
Ibid., pp. 255–294.

14
Ibid., p. 73.

15
Ibid., p. 75.

16
Graham Finney, *Drugs: Administering Catastrophe* (Washington, D.C.: Drug Abuse Council, 1975), p. 17.

17
Alan Altshuler, *The City Planning Process* (Ithaca: Cornell University Press, 1965), pp. 144–188.

18
David Mayhew, *Congress: The Electoral Connection* (New Haven: Yale University Press, 1974), pp. 61–73.

Chapter 5

1
The Manhattan bus route case occurred when I was working in the mayor's office in 1966, and this account is based on my own personal observation of events and on notes I kept in a diary during the period.

2
This account is also based on my personal experience and on my diary of events in the mayor's office in 1966.

3
New York Times, January 12, 1966, p. 17. This account is based on coverage in the *New York Times* and on an analysis of the transit strike in Hentoff, *Political Life.*

4
For a full account of the entire episode at Ocean Hill-Brownsville, see
Barbara Carter, *Pickets, Parents, and Power* (New York: Citation Press,
1971). The account that follows relies heavily on Carter's chronology of
events. For another treatment of Ocean Hill that has been useful in
developing this brief synopsis, see Miriam Wasserman, *The School Fix*
(New York: Outerbridge and Dienstfney, 1970).

5
Ibid., p. 37.

6
Ibid., p. 103.

7
This judgment is based on my own experience in city hall and on
conversations with several mayoral aides.

8
For a detailed analysis of the decentralization movement, see Yates,
Neighborhood Democracy, and Robert Yin and Douglas Yates, *Street-
Level Governments—A Rand Corporation Research Study* (Lexington,
Mass.: D.C. Heath, 1975).

9
These picket signs are pictured on the jacket cover of Carter, *Pickets,
Parents.*

10
Robert L. Crain et al., *The Politics of Community Conflict* (Indianapolis: Bobbs-Merrill, 1969).

11
Ibid., p. 228.

12
Banfield, *Political Influence,* p. 318.

13
Gordon, *City Limits,* pp. 45ff.

14
Ibid., p. 280.

15
James Q. Wilson, "The Mayors vs. the Cities," *The Public Interest,*
no. 16 (Summer 1969): 26.

16
The reference again is to Mayhew, *Congress,* pp. 61–73.

17
Long, *The Polity.*

18

Ibid., p. 142.

19

Ibid., p. 144.

20

Mario Cuomo, *Forest Hills Diary* (New York: Random House, 1974), p. 162.

Chapter 6

1

In my analysis of Lindsay I rely heavily on my own experience in and around city hall in New York. My experience in New York City government is described more fully in the acknowledgments and preface.

2

The saga of Richard C. Lee's regime in New Haven has been told many times. In my analysis I rely on my own lengthy personal conversations with Lee and on discussions that were held in a class we jointly taught at Yale on urban politics. For published material on Lee, I have relied on Dahl, *Who Governs?* and on Raymond E. Wolfinger, *The Politics of Progress* (Englewood Cliffs, N.J.: Prentice-Hall, 1974).

3

Milton Rakove, *Don't Make No Waves . . . Don't Back No Losers* (Bloomington: Indiana University Press, 1975).

4

The Daley literature is by now also quite rich—though most of it is journalistic. For a vivid and critical portrait of Daley, see Mike Royko, *Boss* (New York: Dutton, 1971). For a more sympathetic account, see Len O'Connor, *Clout: Mayor Daley and His City* (Chicago: Henry Regency Company, 1975).

5

For my account of Robert Wagner I rely on personal conversations and on the news-clipping file compiled on New York's mayors by the municipal library in New York City. This file has also provided the central source for my comments on Mayor Beame.

6

This phrase was one of Lindsay's main campaign slogans in 1965. I have discussed it and other aspects of the first Lindsay campaign in my unpublished senior thesis at Yale, "John V. Lindsay and the New York Democracy."

7

Another slogan from Lindsay's 1965 campaign. Murray Kempton first made the comment, and Lindsay used it as an "endorsement."

8
Moscow, *What Have You Done for Me Lately?*

9
See Martin and Susan Tolchin, *To the Victor* (New York: Random House, 1971).

10
For an account of these and other "entrepreneurs," see Jeanne Lowe, *Cities in a Race with Time* (New York: Random House, 1967).

11
For an account of Hatcher's administration in Gary, see James Hoskins, *A Piece of the Power* (New York: Dial Press, 1972), pp. 49–88.

12
This is, of course, the central argument of this book. For corroborating evidence see Hentoff, *Political Life.*

13
One example of this pattern is Lee's development of the redevelopment bureaucracy. Another example is found in Lee's creation of an antipoverty bureaucracy. For an account of this experience, see Russell Murphy, *Political Entrepreneurs* (Lexington, Mass.: D. C. Heath, 1971).

14
See Caro, *Power Broker.*

15
Theodore Lowi, "Machine Politics . . . Old and New," *The Public Interest,* no. 9 (Fall 1967): 83–92.

16
For an analysis of this point, see Yates, *Neighborhood Democracy,* chap. 9.

Chapter 7

1
In 1974–1975 I worked with the development administrator of the city of New Haven on an analysis of alternative strategies for allocating revenue-sharing money. It was difficult to invent useful criteria to serve as priorities for allocation. In any case the press of demands on city hall for money as well as the pervasiveness of political exchange made any attempt at rational policy analysis very hard. I should note also that I worked closely with Donald Kettl in this work for the city of New Haven and owe much of my understanding of the politics of the new federalism to him.

2
Milton Kotler, *Neighborhood Government* (New York: Bobbs-Merrill, 1969), p. 3.

Postscript

1
See Morton Grodzins, *The American System* (Chicago: Rand McNally, 1966).

2
Ibid., and Daniel Elazar, *The American Partnership: Intergovernmental Cooperation in Nineteenth-Century United States* (Chicago: University of Chicago Press, 1962).

3
Grodzins, *American System.*

4
For a detailed analysis of the politics of federal grants, see Pressman, *Federal Programs.* The structure and impact of the two major federal urban interventions in community action and model cities are analyzed in Mel Scott, *American City Planning* (Berkeley: University of California Press, 1969), chap. 8.

5
Pressman, *Federal Programs,* p. 11.

6
Ibid., pp. 7ff.

7
For a thorough study of the structure and functioning of metropolitan governments in America, see John Bollens and Henry Schmandt, *The Metropolis* (New York: Harper & Row, 1965). For a more recent policy analysis of the costs, benefits, and prospects of metropolitan structures, see Steven Erie et al., *Reform of Metropolitan Governments* (Washington, D.C.: Resources for the Future, 1972).

8
See Edward Sofen, *The Miami Metropolitan Experiment* (Bloomington: Indiana University Press, 1963).

9
Mark Gelfand, *A Nation of Cities* (New York: Oxford University Press, 1975).

10
Charles Tiebout, "A Pure Theory of Local Expenditures," *Journal of Political Economy,* October 1956.

11
See Martin, *Cities and the Federal System,* chap. 3.

12
For a useful overview, see Leigh Grosenick, ed., *The Administration of the New Federalism,* American Society for Public Administration, Special Publication (September 1973).

Index